Facework

SAGE SERIES ON CLOSE RELATIONSHIPS

Series Editors
Clyde Hendrick, Ph.D., and
Susan S. Hendrick, Ph.D.

Facework

William R. Cupach
Sandra Metts

SS
CR
Sage
Series
on Close
Relationships

SAGE Publications
International Educational and Professional Publisher
Thousand Oaks   London   New Delhi

For information address:

SAGE Publications, Inc.
2455 Teller Road
Thousand Oaks, California 91320

SAGE Publications Ltd.
6 Bonhill Street
London EC2A 4PU
United Kingdom

SAGE Publications India Pvt. Ltd.
M-32 Market
Greater Kailash I
New Delhi 110 048 India

Printed in the United States of America

Library of Congress Cataloging-in-Publication Data

Cupach, William R.
    Facework / authors, William R. Cupach, Sandra Metts.
        p.   cm.—(Sage series on close relationships)
    Includes bibliographical references and index.
    ISBN 0-8039-4711-9.—ISBN 0-8039-4712-7 (pbk.)
    1. Interpersonal relations. 2. Interpersonal communication.
    3. Interpersonal conflict. 4. Self-presentation. 5. Social skills.
    I. Metts, Sandra. II. Title. III. Series.
    HM132.C86   1994
    302—dc20   94-4600

94 95 96 97 98   10 9 8 7 6 5 4 3 2 1

Sage Production Editor: Yvonne Könneker

Contents

Series Editors' Introduction

W hen we first began our work on love attitudes more than a decade ago, we did not know what to call our research area. In some ways it represented an extension of earlier work in interpersonal attraction. Most of our scholarly models were psychologists (though sociologists had long been deeply involved in the areas of courtship and marriage), yet we sometimes felt as if our work had no professional "home." That has all changed. Our research not only has a home, it has an extended family as well, and the family is composed of relationship researchers. Over the past decade the discipline of close relationships (also called personal relationships and intimate relationships) has emerged, developed, and flourished.

Two aspects of close relationships research should be noted. The first is its rapid growth, resulting in numerous books, journals, handbooks, book series, and professional organizations. As fast as the field grows, however, the demand for even more research and knowledge seems to be ever increasing. Questions about close, personal relationships still far exceed answers. The second noteworthy aspect of the new discipline of close relationships is its interdisciplinary nature. The field owes its vitality to scholars from communication, family studies and human development, psychology (clinical, counseling, developmental, social), and sociology as well as other disciplines such as nursing and social work. It is this interdisciplinary wellspring that gives close relationships research its diversity and richness, qualities that we hope to achieve in the current series.

The **Sage Series on Close Relationships** is designed to acquaint diverse readers with the most up-to-date information about various topics in close relationships theory and research. Each volume in the series covers a particular topic or theme in one area of close relationships. Each book reviews the particular topic area, describes contemporary research in the area (including the authors' own work, where appropriate), and offers some suggestions for interesting research questions and/or real-world applications related to the topic. The volumes are designed to be appropriate for students and professionals in communication, family studies, psychology, sociology, and social work, among others. A basic assumption of the series is that the broad panorama of close relationships can best be portrayed by authors from multiple disciplines, so that the series cannot be "captured" by any single disciplinary bias.

The current book, called simply *Facework*, is the first series volume with a clear communication orientation. Authors William Cupach and Sandra Metts review their own research and that of others on the self-presentational aspects of communication in intimate relationships. Gaining face, maintaining face, and losing face all have numerous implications for the management of close relationships, and these two communication scholars make a compelling case for facework as basic relationship currency. Whether our relationships are in stages of formation, maintenance, or disengagement, we are (or should be) attending to the face needs of ourselves and our partners. The book is exceedingly readable; its clear and humorous prose offers the reader a pleasurable learning experience. Perhaps that is to be expected from two experts in communication.

CLYDE HENDRICK
SUSAN S. HENDRICK
SERIES EDITORS

Preface

This book is about the concepts of *face* and *facework*. Our goal is to show the centrality of face issues in the conduct of close relationships by extending and amplifying face management theory. We believe these concepts are useful for understanding certain aspects of the everyday functioning of close relationships. In particular, we find the management of face to be useful for illuminating how relational partners cope with problematic and challenging interaction episodes.

In the opening chapter, we delineate the concepts of face and facework and explain their relevance to social interaction and personal relationships. Chapter 2 characterizes the prototypical problematic episode—the embarrassing social predicament. We suggest that coping with embarrassing situations helps individuals to learn the social expectations and practices associated with managing threats to face. Chapter 3 addresses face concerns that arise in developing relationships. We specifically consider how partners manage vulnerability as informational and physical intimacy increase. An important theme in Chapter 3 is that partners construct a shared relational culture different from, but based on, social norms and expectations. In Chapter 4, we consider the management of problematic episodes by partners in established close relationships. We examine the problematic episodes of complaining, seeking or rendering social support, and discovering or revealing a relational transgression. The focus in Chapter 5 shifts to the role of facework in the disengagement and dissolution of close relationships. The final chapter crystallizes some key implications that derive from application of face management theory to close relationships.

We are grateful to the editors of this series, Clyde Hendrick and Susan Hendrick, for their generous patience and guidance throughout this project. We also want to acknowledge our very special friends, Sam and George, who have taught us more than anyone about close relationships, and about ourselves.

WILLIAM R. CUPACH
SANDRA METTS

1

Face Management in
Interpersonal Relationships

"I was so embarrassed!" Have you ever found yourself recounting a story of how you stumbled and fell while trying to impress a new date with your dancing talents? Have you ever expressed in much more somber tones a time when you felt great shame because you violated a trust that you and your partner shared about sexual exclusivity? If you have felt embarrassment, or shame, then you have experienced the effects of *losing face*. If, on the other hand, you have felt pride, or validation, or respect, then you have experienced the effects of *sustaining face*, even, perhaps, during awkward situations. This book is about gaining and losing face in close relationships. The notion of face, and related concepts, is used to explain the role of communication in managing the course of interpersonal relationships.

When Erving Goffman introduced the term *face* in his writings of the 1950s and 1960s, he was not thinking particularly about how it functioned in close relationships. In fact, he was a sociologist whose interest lay primarily in what he called "public performance." He used the metaphor of a play or dramatic enactment to explain how social "actors" performed roles and coordinated their interactions. He proposed a sort of cooperative principle whereby people agree tacitly to support each other's performance or face. To not support each other's face is to disrupt the entire scene, because no one can continue in performance when others are embarrassed or shamed (i.e., out of face).

For some time, the writings of Goffman were taught in sociology courses and used primarily as a way to explain features of public interactions, such as deference and demeanor, impression management, embarrassment, storytelling, and conversational patterns. However, implicit in Goffman's work is the notion that face is fundamental to a sense of self, even in intimate interactions that are not guided by conventionalized norms. Paradoxically, the complexity of managing face is increased for partners in close relationships because familiarity entails some degree of exemption from the obligation to create and support face during private interactions. Thus part of the reason a couple defines itself as intimate is that the need to "perform," in Goffman's sense of performance, is considered unnecessary; yet in this very act of dropping pretense arises the probability of threatening each other's face and, ultimately, sense of social competence.

Most of the time, couples strike a comfortable balance between the extremes of total disregard for face and rigid adherence to formality. They tease each other, but do so gently, and they avoid teasing about sensitive topics. They recognize the need to provide social support and comforting that restores a loss of face. And in general, this is all done without much conscious thought. Few couples sit at the dinner table and talk about their face needs.

However, as automatic and unconscious as these processes may be on a daily basis, face concerns can become acutely prominent when relational partners experience awkward or difficult communication situations. These *problematic* situations represent key turning points in the development of interpersonal relationships. They also offer the greatest opportunities for one or both relational partners to experience a *loss of face*. Consequently, the manner in which problematic situations are managed has implications for the quality and longevity of relationships and for the psychological health of relational partners.

This chapter is devoted to defining key concepts related to face and the processes surrounding face management. In subsequent chapters we will utilize these concepts to explore a variety of problematic situations arising in relationships, ranging from the negotiation of sexual intimacy to breaking up.

❧ Communication and the Management of Face

Face and Face Needs

The conception of self that each person displays in particular interactions with others is called *face*. When a person interacts with another, he or she tacitly presents a conception of who he or she is in that encounter, and seeks confirmation for that conception. In other words, the individual offers an identity that he or she wants to assume and wants others to accept. In social scientific terms, face refers to "socially situated identities people claim or attribute to others" (Tracy, 1990, p. 210).

According to Goffman (1967), whatever the context in which communication occurs, and whatever the relationship shared by interactants, it is assumed that each person's face is supported and maintained during interaction. Out of *self-respect*, communicators are emotionally invested in the presentation and preservation of their own face; out of *considerateness*, communicators exert effort to save the feelings and maintain the face of other people. Goffman characterizes an individual who can experience his or her own face loss without distress as "shameless" and an individual who can unfeelingly observe others lose face as "heartless."

Under normal circumstances, then, individuals reciprocate face support and cooperate to ensure that each other's face is protected. Indeed, when any person's face is threatened during an interaction, all participants are motivated to restore it because not doing so leaves them open to the discomfort and embarrassment that arises from a disrupted interaction.

This mutual cooperation in the maintenance of face is so ordinary and pervasive that it is considered a taken-for-granted principle of interaction. People do it automatically—unless the intent is to embarrass someone playfully or to discredit someone contemptuously. Generally, face is not a conscious concern of communicators. The everyday goals of expressing one's beliefs, ingratiating others, seeking advice, eliciting information, and so on "are typically pursued in such a way as to be consistent with the maintenance of face" (Goffman, 1967, p. 12).

Thus maintaining face is an underlying motive in all social encounters, but it is not usually a strategic objective. It is only when some event, action, or comment discredits face or threatens to discredit face that strategies to minimize the occurrence and consequences of face threat come into consciousness. The next subsection deals with face threats and ways of coping with them.

Threats to Face

Face threats occur when a person's desired identity in a particular interaction is challenged. Given that it is virtually impossible to avoid all face threats at all times, any interaction is *potentially face-threatening* (Tracy, 1990). Even the most skillful and well-intended communicator sometimes finds him- or herself in the position of having spoken an inappropriate comment or having felt diminished by receiving a complaint or criticism from someone else. And as we will see later, some types of interaction episodes, such as terminating a relationship, are by their very nature face-involving situations.

A particularly interesting explication of how face is threatened is offered by Penelope Brown and Stephen Levinson (1987). Drawing from their analysis of 13 societies in various areas of the world, they present a theory based on two types of universal face needs: positive face needs and negative face needs. *Positive face* refers to the desire to be liked and respected by the significant people in our lives. Positive face is supported when messages communicate value for the things we value, appreciation for us as competent individuals, and solidarity with us (Lim & Bowers, 1991). Positive face is threatened when one's fellowship is devalued or one's abilities are questioned. *Negative face* pertains to the desire to be free from constraint and imposition. Messages respecting one's autonomy are supportive of negative face, whereas messages interfering with one's desired actions are threatening to negative face.

Brown and Levinson's description of positive and negative face is interesting because of the dilemma it exposes for people trying to meet both types of face needs for themselves and other people. Essentially, the dilemma is that satisfying one type of face need often threatens the other. Consider this just within an *individual*. Karen Tracy (1990) gives an example of a college professor who values teaching very highly and wants to cultivate his students' potential. However, the cost of this desire is that students make daily demands on his time and drain his energy. His positive face needs are satisfied at the cost of his negative face needs.

To understand this dilemma at the *relationship level*, think for a moment about what you do when you like someone: You spend time with the person, teasing and complimenting, self-disclosing, borrowing money or clothes; you drop by the person's home unexpectedly, and so forth. You do what comes naturally when you care about and value someone. You are, in these behaviors, showing regard for the individual's positive face. However, consider how these actions might threaten negative face. This other person may feel it an imposition to have to stop his or her activity to visit with you, or may not be comfortable with your self-disclosures, or may find it tiring to entertain you when he or she would prefer to do something else. These responses are natural because your friend's negative face is being constrained *at the very same time* his or her positive face is being validated. In fact, sometimes your own negative face may feel threatened because you simply don't want to be pleasant, or funny, or supportive toward your friend; you may even want to be free of the sense of obligation that the friendship implies. Leslie Baxter (1988) eloquently captures the dialectical nature of these competing forces:

> No relationship can exist by definition unless the parties sacrifice some individual autonomy. However, too much connection para-doxically destroys the relationship because the individual identities become lost (Askham, 1976). Simultaneously, an individual's auton-omy can be conceptualized only in terms of separation from others. But too much autonomy paradoxically destroys the individual's identity, because connections with others are the "stuff" of which identity is made (Lock, 1986). (p. 259)

The dilemma of satisfying positive and negative face at the same time may seem like a no-win situation, but it is not. It is a matter of balancing the natural tension between being connected to some-one and being independent. As we will discuss below, facework and politeness are communication mechanisms that allow us to manage this dilemma.

Facework

Facework is communication designed to counteract face threats to self and others (Goffman, 1967). On many occasions, face-threatening acts can be avoided or minimized before they occur through the use of *preventive facework*. On other occasions, face threats are not anticipated and the loss of face must be remediated through *corrective facework*. We will spend the next few pages discussing each of these types of facework. We then close this chapter with discussion of a third type of facework unique to close relationships that is contained in a couple's *personal idioms*.

Preventive facework. Avoiding face threat is often accomplished by such tactics as avoiding face-threatening topics, changing the subject of conversation when it appears to be moving in a face-threatening direction, and pretending not to notice when something face-threatening has been said or done. In addition, individuals employ linguistic devices such as "disclaimers" (Hewitt & Stokes, 1975) and "politeness" (Brown & Levinson, 1987) to minimize the negative implications that might be made about them when they know they are about to threaten someone's face.

Disclaimers are statements people use to minimize the negative attributions that might be ascribed to their motives or character because they are about to violate expectations for appropriate behavior. Hewitt and Stokes (1975) identify five types of disclaimers:

1. *hedging:* indicates uncertainty and receptivity to suggestions ("I may be wrong, but . . . ")
2. *credentialing:* indicates that there are good reasons and appropriate qualifications for engaging in a sanctionable action ("I'm your husband; I have every right to read your mail.")
3. *sin license:* indicates that this is an acceptable occasion for rule violation and should not be taken as a character defect ("What the hell, this is a special occasion.")
4. *cognitive disclaimer:* indicates that the impending behavior is reasonable and under cognitive control, in spite of appearances ("I know this sounds crazy, but . . . ")
5. *appeal for suspended judgment:* request to withhold judgment for a possibly offensive act until it has been fully explained ("Hear me out before you get upset.")

In essence, disclaimers are used by speakers to save their own face; they signal a message something like, "Please recognize that I am aware of social appropriateness and I ask your indulgence while I act inappropriately; I am not merely rude or stupid." Politeness strategies, on the other hand, are more directly focused on the face of the recipient of the threat. They signal a message something like, "Please recognize that I regard your face needs very highly and would not threaten them if it were not necessary to do so; I am not merely selfish and insensitive to your needs."

Politeness strategies allow people to walk a fine line between being totally indirect and possibly never getting their point across (e.g., "Gee, there's a great movie playing downtown tonight . . . hmm, well, hope you enjoy it"), and being unexpectedly blunt and direct (e.g., "Take me to the movie tonight because I want to see it"). Very intimate partners can be a bit more indirect than social acquaintances because they are attuned to each other's hints. And intimate partners can be a bit more direct than social acquaintances because they know that the relationship is based on mutual positive regard even when it is not demonstrated in one or two particular interactions. However, frequent and repeated disregard for each other's face may eventually lead a couple to feel the foundation of mutual regard in their relationship may be weakening.

Thus it is no accident that people have developed an elaborate system of politeness strategies to use when they want to reach a goal efficiently but do not want to appear insensitive to the face concerns of the other person. Brown and Levinson (1987) describe the general strategies of positive and negative politeness that are respectively directed toward the positive and negative face needs of the partner. Positive politeness expresses appreciation for the value of another person and expresses affiliation with that person. Positive politeness includes messages showing that the partner's desires are known and considered to be important, that he or she is viewed as a member of an in-group, a friend, or a valued other. For instance: "Hey buddy! You're really doin' great in calculus class. How 'bout sharing some of your talent with me?" Negative politeness offers assurances that the partner's freedom will not be unnecessarily curtailed and that he or she has options. These messages are characterized by self-effacement and formality, permitting the partner to feel that his or her response was not obligatory or coerced. For example: "John, I hate to bother you, but if you are not too busy, would it be possible to get a lift to campus?"

Corrective facework. In an effort to repair face damage that has occurred because of a transgression, corrective facework is employed. Corrective behaviors may be *defensively* offered by the actor responsible for creating face threat, may be *protectively* offered by other people who witness the loss of face, or may be offered by the person who has lost face as he or she attempts to regain lost social identity.

The facts that facework can be performed by observers and participants, that it can be accepted or rejected, and that its effec-

tiveness depends on the features of a particular situation underscore how challenging problematic events can be. The restoration
of lost face and the smooth realignment of a disrupted episode are
truly cooperative accomplishments. We describe below several
types of strategies used during the remediation process. Although
we present them separately, it is important to remember that
people often use several of them in various orderings as the
process of restoring face unfolds (Cupach & Metts, 1990).

   A large class of behaviors intended to contain or control the
extent of damage to face is called *avoidance*. The principle underlying avoidance is that in some face-threatening situations, drawing explicit attention to the face threat may be counterproductive.
If only one's own face has been modestly threatened but the faces
of others remain largely intact, then the benefit of saving one's
own face might be at the expense of threatening the face of others
(Cupach & Metts, 1990). Belaboring a minor infraction can create
inconvenience for others and possibly induce them to feel embarrassment. Similarly, if an observer notes that one has committed
an error, he or she may overlook it. People routinely gloss over
their own and each other's mistakes when they are relatively
minor. This is accomplished by acting as if face has not been
threatened. Gracefully continuing with social interaction following a minor predicament demonstrates one's poise and minimizes
the extent to which other people become embarrassed or annoyed.
Of course, when abashment is intense, one may exhibit an extreme
form of avoidance by physically fleeing the embarrassing or shame-
ful encounter (Cupach, Metts, & Hazleton, 1986).

   Humor is frequently a response to predicaments, partly because
some predicaments are intended to be comical (such as teasing;
Argyle, Furnham, & Graham, 1981; Knapp, Stafford, & Daly, 1986;
Sharkey, 1991) and some are inherently funny in their consequences.
Argyle et al. (1981) found, for example, that rule-breaking episodes
are characterized by a fundamental underlying dimension ranging from humorous to irritating. Similarly, affective reactions to
rule-breaking episodes are characterized by the dimension of
laughter versus anger. If the face-threatening event involves a
harmless accident or flub, then laughter allows the release of

nervous tension and signals that the problematic circumstances need not be taken too seriously. Making a joke can show that the offending person acknowledges blameworthiness (as with a simple excuse or apology) and can also allow the person to demonstrate poise and social competence (Edelmann, 1985; Fink & Walker, 1977).

Apologies admit blame and seek atonement for untoward behavior (Goffman, 1967; Schlenker, 1980; Tedeschi & Riess, 1981). The form of an apology can range from a simple statement, such as "I'm sorry," to more elaborate forms including one or more of the following elements: (a) expression of regret or remorse, (b) requests for forgiveness, (c) self-castigation, (d) promises not to repeat the transgression in the future, and (e) offers of restitution (Goffman, 1971; Schlenker & Darby, 1981).

The nonverbal display of anxiety or discomfort can function much like an apology insofar as it demonstrates to others that the offending person acknowledges the impropriety of his or her own behavior. Merely appearing to be chagrined (by blushing or grimacing) can show one's self-effacement and thereby mitigate negative attributions that might be ascribed by observers (Castelfranchi & Poggi, 1990; Edelmann, 1982; Semin & Manstead, 1982).

Accounts are verbal explanations given to *explain* inappropriate or awkward behavior (Buttny, 1985, 1987; Scott & Lyman, 1968). Two general classes of accounts are excuses and justifications. *Excuses* attempt to minimize the actor's responsibility for an event ("I didn't mean it"; "I couldn't help it"; "It's not my fault"); *justifications* reframe an event by downplaying its negative implications ("It's not so bad"; "It's for your own good"). There are numerous varieties of excuses and justifications. Several authors have described a wide range of types of excuses and justifications (Schlenker, 1980; Schonbach, 1980, 1990; Scott & Lyman, 1968; Snyder, Higgins, & Stuckey, 1983; Tedeschi & Riess, 1981). Examples from the synthesized typology of Semin and Manstead (1983) are given in Table 1.1.

Physical remediation involves behavioral (nonverbal) correction or repair of physical damage (if any has occurred) associated with a loss of face. This includes such acts as adjusting clothing (zip-

Table 1.1 A Typology of Accounts

Excuses
    Denial of intent
        "It was an accident."
        "I didn't know you would take my remark personally."
    Denial of volition
        "I was extremely tired."
        "I can't approve your request; I don't have the authority."
    Denial of agency
        "It wasn't me."
        "I don't remember anything about it."
        "I wasn't the only one who did it."
    Appeal to mitigating circumstances
        "Jane pressured me to do it."

Justifications
    Claim that effect has been misrepresented
        "No harm done."
    Appeal to principle of retribution
        "He got what he deserved!"
    Social comparison
        "Other people get away with it."
    Appeal to higher authority
        "My boss ordered me to do it."
    Self-fulfillment
        "It allowed me to vent my anger."
        "I did it because I thought it was morally right."
    Appeal to utilitarianism
        "In the long run, the benefits will outweigh the harm."
    Appeal to values
        "I did it out of a sense of loyalty."
        "It was the fair thing to do."
    Appeal to need for facework
        "I wanted to appear credible."

SOURCE: Adapted from Semin and Manstead (1983). Used by permission.

ping up one's pants), cleaning up a spill, and fixing a broken toy (Metts & Cupach, 1989b; Semin & Manstead, 1982; Sharkey & Stafford, 1990).

Most of the remedial facework strategies employed by a person creating face loss can also be utilized by observers on the person's behalf. Observers can offer physical assistance following a pratfall, and can make various types of positive comments to assist a face-threatened individual, including attribution of guilt or responsibility for the occurrence of the event to persons other than the embarrassed person, positive comments on the embarrassed person's conduct during the failure event (e.g., expressing understanding, appeasement, friendly advice), and positive comments on the embarrassed person's liability for the consequences of the failure event (exoneration, waiving of claims, pardon, compassion, offers of help) (Schonbach, 1990). Humor is also a common strategy, although it entails some risk, as the inferred line between laughing "with" the person and laughing "at" him or her can be blurry (Cupach & Metts, 1990). Similarly, attempts to avoid calling attention to an untoward act are expected, particularly for minor infractions. However, such inattention can exacerbate discomfort on some occasions. By not overtly attempting to repair the awkward encounter, individuals remain somewhat uncertain about whether or not they have demonstrated efforts commensurate with expectations to repair face.

Observers also have unique remedial responses at their disposal that can be particularly effective in diminishing the discomfort felt by the person who has lost face. In fact, one study found that observers were much more effective than transgressors in ameliorating the transgressor's embarrassment following a face-threatening predicament (see Cupach & Metts, 1990). In particular, observers can offer help by expressing *empathy*, communicating to the distressed person that his or her predicament is not unique or uncommon. They can also offer *support* through indications of positive regard in spite of the predicament. We found in one study that approximately half of all remedial responses offered by observers were such displays of empathy and support (Metts & Cupach, 1989b).

The Aggravation-Mitigation Continuum

Whether enacted by a face-threatened individual or an observer, responses to face-threatening events can be located theoretically on a continuum of *aggravation-mitigation* (Cody & McLaughlin,

1985; Labov & Fanshel, 1977). Aggravating behaviors are aggressive, challenging, inflammatory, and generally escalate or exacerbate face threat. Contempt for face, or at least a lack of respect for face, is implied by aggravating behaviors. Mitigating moves are relatively more deferential or conciliatory, and generally attempt to minimize face threat. Honor and respect toward face is implied by mitigating moves.

We specify the theoretical nature of the aggravation-mitigation continuum because, in reality, almost any message could fall anywhere on the continuum, depending upon the situation. In situations where a person wants to escalate conflict, for example, even the most deferential comment can be interpreted aggressively. Consider a married couple who have been arguing over how to discipline one of the children. When the husband finally says, "Okay, okay, we'll do it your way because of course you always know best," the wife takes that as a sarcastic and inflammatory remark. That same statement between a married couple who are doing their income taxes may be an honest appraisal that one person really does know more about finances and his or her approach to doing taxes is best for both. So to say that messages are aggravating or mitigating is misleading unless it is noted that such a statement is a shorthand way of saying that in certain situations certain messages are interpreted as aggravating or as mitigating.

Personal Idioms

One type of facework is generally not even considered facework at all—at least not in the technical sense in which we use the term in the previous section. However, there is a strong element of face management in the personal idioms that intimate couples create and use on a daily basis. Robert Bell and his colleagues asked people in all types of relationships to describe any private codes or phrases they used with each other that other people wouldn't understand (Bell, Buerkel-Rothfuss, & Gore, 1987; Bell & Healey, 1992; Hopper, Knapp, & Scott, 1981). The respondents reported hundreds of such phrases, which the researchers sorted into categories based on their

Table 1.2 Functions and Examples of Personal Idioms

Confrontations	to express displeasure with partner's behavior (e.g., using "Jello-Bitch" to inform the female partner that she is being obnoxious; pulling on the partner's nose when criticism gets out of hand)
Expression of affection	to express love, give reassurance to, or praise partner (e.g., using the words "luscious" or "huggle" to say "I love you"; aggressively sucking the partner's chin to express caring)
Labels for outsiders	nicknames for other individuals or groups of people (e.g., calling a friend of the couple "Pennis" when his real name is Ennis; referring to a neighbor who plays music too loudly as the "Funkmaster")
Nicknames	terms of address used exclusively by the couple (e.g., "Pookers," "Applehead," "Fifi")
Requests	to request some form of action (e.g., asking "How ya doin'?" at social gatherings to express a need to talk to the partner in private; saying "L.L."—abbreviation for "Let's leave"—to let partner know you wish to leave a party)
Sexual invitations	to propose sexual activity (e.g., saying things like "I want some ice cream" or "My ears are popping" to initiate sex; using the phrase "My beef's on hard" and "The river is flowing" to encourage a transition from foreplay to sexual intercourse)
Sexual references and euphemisms	to make reference to genitals, breasts, intercourse, birth control, and sexual techniques (e.g., referring to breasts as Bullwinkle and Rocky; calling oral sex "torture")
Teasing insults	to derogate one's partner, usually in a spirit of play (e.g., calling partner "Hogmo" to refer to his poor table manners; using "wimpatus" to refer to the partner when he or she is afraid of doing something)

SOURCE: Bell et al. (1987).

functions. The eight categories that emerged are listed and explained in Table 1.2.

An examination of these categories reveals how they function as face-saving strategies. Consider the teasing insult, for example. If a college student says to his friend, "It must be nice to own a bar stool down at Rocky's," he can indicate to his friend in a teasing way that he is concerned about his drinking without explicitly calling his face into question. For a dating couple, sexual euphemisms and routines can allow them to express the desire to have sex without threatening each other's negative face or express the desire not to have sex without threatening each other's positive face. In short, personal idioms are a brilliant way for couples to manage the pulls toward conflicting goals in a very efficient way.

❧ The Importance of Facework in Interpersonal Relationships

For several reasons, the management of face is particularly relevant to the formation and erosion of interpersonal relationships. First, the ability to manage one's own and others' face is fundamental to interpersonal competence (Cupach & Imahori, 1993a; Weinstein, 1969; Wiemann, 1977). In order for people to achieve their own goals, they must be able to establish and maintain desired identities for each other when they interact. Succinctly stated, getting ahead ordinarily entails getting along, which in turn necessitates sensitivity to the face needs of others. As Goffman (1967) suggests, in our society, the ability to engage in appropriate facework is tantamount to "tact, *savoir-faire*, diplomacy, or social skill" (p. 13).

Second, face support is identity confirming. Situational identities constitute important sources of rewards and costs for social actors (Weinstein, 1969). The importance of confirmation is magnified as the intimacy of the relationship between partners escalates. Indeed, Weinstein (1969) contends that "it is only in the most impersonal encounters that the situational identities of the parties are not a principal nexus of rewards and costs. Often, they are precisely and completely that" (p. 757).

Third, effective facework fosters mutual respect and buttresses against contempt (see Penman, 1990). This supports the ritual order of social interactions, allowing encounters between people to be relatively smooth and enjoyable, rather than disruptive and distressing. Moreover, facework is integral to managing the challenges and

dilemmas of relationships. At its best, effective face support per-
mits us to achieve (however fleeting) relationship nirvana. At its
worst, persistent face loss can create bitter enmity and personal
agony.

ﻩ Preview of Subsequent Chapters

In the following chapters, we explore the dynamics of face and
facework in problematic situations routinely encountered by relationship partners. We have chosen episodes that are often particularly consequential for relational participants and their relationships,
and we have selected a variety of problematic contexts in order to
demonstrate the relevance of face and its management across the
full life span of relationships. In Chapter 2, we discuss the prototypical problematic episode—the embarrassing social predicament. In coping with embarrassment, individuals learn the social
expectations and practices for managing face threat. Remedial
processes in embarrassing predicaments are the foundation for
the particularized strategies of facework that are adapted to problematic episodes within close relationships. In Chapters 3, 4, and
5 we explore the manifestation of face management during the
development and maintenance of relationship intimacy, as well as
during the termination of close relationships. The final chapter
offers a summary and synthesis of the operation of facework in
close relationships.

2

Embarrassing Predicaments

Professor Edward Gross tells the story of a foreign diplomat attending an afternoon reception. As he was getting up to leave, he noticed that his fly was partially open.

> He sheepishly retreated to the couch to zip up, but in the process caught his tie in his fly. The hostess, noticing something amiss, offered her help. The diplomat, not wanting to draw attention to his predicament, shooed her away. The diplomat resumed efforts to untangle himself. But with every jerk of his head, the knot tightened, and his face turned blue. A crowd gathered around him. Finally, the hostess got a pair of scissors and snipped off the tie. As the diplomat rushed out the door, a piece of cloth wafted through the air. (*Daily Pantagraph*, June 7, 1992, p. C1)

All people, including socially skilled ones, inevitably are confronted with embarrassing predicaments. Who, after all, has not botched a social performance at some time? Virtually everyone has been held accountable at times for behaving contrary to the expectations of others. Social predicaments constitute problematic situations because they threaten the identities that individuals desire to portray, and consequently lead to a temporary break-down in the ordinarily smooth and routine contours of social interaction.

This chapter explores embarrassing predicaments as a type of problematic social situation in which facework is critical (e.g., Edelmann, 1987; Gonzales, Pederson, Manning, & Wetter, 1991; Modigliani, 1968; Petronio, 1984). In addition to describing the types of circumstances creating embarrassment and, concomi-tantly, loss of face, we consider the means by which interactants utilize facework to manage such encounters effectively.

ﾞ The Nature of Embarrassing Predicaments

Embarrassing predicaments are problematic social situations characterized by awkwardness or difficulty (Silver, Sabini, & Par-rott, 1987). They occur when individuals are perceived to have acted incompetently, that is, when behavior is judged to be inap-propriate, ineffective, or foolish. Such behavior ordinarily dam-ages the identity one prefers to exhibit in the company of others. In the terminology of Goffman (1967), predicaments engender undesirable symbolic implications that threaten face. They are face-threatening for the individual caught in the predicament because he or she believes that an unwanted image of the self has been projected to others. Predicaments are face-threatening to others to the extent they feel they have been imposed upon and/or the events are seen to reflect badly on their own self-images. The uncomfortable feelings of deficiency, abashment, and discombobu-lation that result from impaired identities are called *embarrassment*.

The individual who performs behavior creating embarrassment may or may not correspond to the individual who feels embarrass-ment, or the person for whom embarrassment is felt. For example, suppose Vince, Tim, and John are engaged in social conversation.

Tim unintentionally insults Vince. Tim may feel embarrassed for committing the faux pas. As well, Vince may experience chagrin for being insulted, whether or not Tim is embarrassed. It is also possible that Vince is embarrassed *for* Tim, whose inappropriate behavior has been witnessed by John. Sensing the awkwardness of the situation and the discomfort experienced by Tim (or Vince), John may also feel "empathic" embarrassment for Tim and/or Vince. Any combination of these experiences of embarrassment is possible, even though Tim is responsible for initially creating the predicament.

Types of Predicaments

Embarrassing predicaments encompass a wide range of events, such as pratfalls and gaffes, flubs and faux pas, boners and blunders, miscues and mistakes. Several researchers have developed category schemes to characterize the types of circumstances giving rise to embarrassing predicaments (e.g., Cupach & Metts, 1990; Gross & Stone, 1964; Miller, 1992; Modigliani, 1968; Sharkey & Stafford, 1990; Weinberg, 1968). Reviews of these schemes are offered by Miller (1986) and Edelmann (1987). Buss (1980), for example, identifies five specific types of events that commonly cause embarrassment:

1. impropriety (e.g., improper dress, dirty talk)
2. lack of competence (e.g., a failure of social graces)
3. conspicuousness (e.g., being singled out for attention by others)
4. breach of privacy (e.g., invasion of personal space or undesired leakage of emotion)
5. overpraise (e.g., receiving more acclaim than is deserved)

An important feature to consider when classifying embarrassing predicaments is who caused the event to occur (Sharkey & Stafford, 1990). In a classification of more than 3,000 embarrassing events, Sattler (1965) identifies five general categories reflecting the possible relationships between the person who feels embarrassed and the person creating the embarrassment:

1. P (the embarrassed person) is the agent.
2. P places O (another person) in a negative position.
3. P is the recipient of O's behavior.
4. O does something that reflects on P.
5. P is embarrassed for O.

The first two of these categories concern embarrassment experienced as a result of behavior performed by the embarrassed person, perhaps the more common (and more frequently studied) form of embarrassment. The other three categories defined by Sattler pertain to embarrassment experienced by a person as a consequence of the actions of another.

Based upon a synthesis of recent research on the types of events leading to embarrassment (Cupach & Imahori, 1993b; Cupach & Metts, 1992; Imahori & Cupach, 1991; Miller, 1992), we propose 12 categories of predicaments. These events can be divided into self-induced embarrassment and embarrassment created by others.

Self-Induced Embarrassing Predicaments

Accidents involve a loss of comportment, such as tripping, falling, farting, or belching. These incidents, although potentially mildly offensive to others, are unintentional and generally only threaten the face of the person committing the awkward behavior. *Mistakes* occur when a person misinterprets a situation and unintentionally commits a faux pas, such as walking into the wrong room or saying something stupid or incorrect. The person committing a mistake usually suffers some face loss; others may be moderately offended or relatively unaffected. *Conspicuousness* arises when a person draws unwanted attention from others. This typically stems from misbehaving in public, such as having a private argument in public. *Inept performance* creates embarrassment for a person who fails to display an expected skill or ability. Examples include giving a poor performance at a musical audition or flunking a driver's examination. *Tactlessness* consists of unintentionally offending others through carelessness. Saying insulting things about another person and not realizing the insulted person can hear the remarks is an example of tactlessness. *Deliberate rule violation* entails breaching the prescriptive expectations of others and getting caught. Being caught in a lie and sneaking a cigarette in a nonsmoking area are examples.

Predicaments Created by Others

Awkward interaction involves circumstances in which an individual experiences a loss of script regarding how to proceed in an ongoing interaction, or feels uncomfortable as a result of possessing guilty knowledge of a past incident. *Team embarrassment* is feeling guilty by virtue of being associated with another who is behaving inappropriately. One can feel embarrassed about the obnoxious behavior of a friend owing to the possibility that negative attributions about the friend may be generalized to oneself. *Individualization* occurs when one is the public recipient of praise, criticism, sanctions, or teasing from others. *Caused to look unpoised* occurs when another intentionally or unintentionally makes a person look foolish or discombobulated, such as by spilling a drink on the person. *Rudeness* or *abusiveness* occurs when one is ridiculed or treated with disdain or disrespect. Being *falsely accused* or *implicated* would include incidents such as inadvertently stumbling on a crime scene just prior to the police arriving. *Privacy violation* results when personal, secret information is revealed to another. *Empathic embarrassment* occurs when one observes another to behave foolishly or inappropriately, and consequently feels abashed for that person (Miller, 1987).

The Severity of Predicaments

Clearly, one of the most important features characterizing a predicament is its severity. Predicaments can range in seriousness from a minor faux pas to a grave moral breach. The relative severity of a predicament is based upon two principal factors: the undesirability of the event and the person's apparent responsibility for the event (Schlenker, 1980; Snyder, 1985). The greater the undesirability and the greater the attributed responsibility, the more severe the predicament. These two factors parallel the fundamental dimensions that people use to appraise behavior, that is, the valence of an act and a person's linkage to the act (Snyder & Higgins, 1990).

The negative repercussions of a predicament occur in two primary domains. First, undesirability of an action can be judged in terms of the emotional effects on the person. The affective consequences of predicaments range from amusement to anger, from mild and fleeting chagrin to intense and enduring shame or guilt. Most commonly, predicaments are associated with feelings of embarrassment (Edelmann, 1987). The more personally distressing a predicament is for a person, the more severe it is. The severity of a predicament for a person will be in direct proportion to his or her perceived degree of face loss.

The aversive nature of predicaments stems principally from the negative attributions ascribed to a person who has behaved inappropriately. Getting caught in a predicament potentially casts aspersions on one's character or social competence. Thus a person's reaction to a predicament is intimately tied to the perceived expectations and exhibited reactions of observers (e.g., Argyle et al., 1981).

Undesirability is also judged with respect to the impact of the predicament on others. As the negative consequences for others intensify, so does the severity of the predicament. Thus causing embarrassment, inconvenience, annoyance, aggravation, or offense for others exacerbates the severity of the predicament for the offender. In short, to threaten the face of others is to undermine one's own face.

Both actual responsibility and attributed responsibility for predicaments vary considerably. Goffman (1967) notes that some incidents are innocent and unwitting; others are incidental in that the transgression is anticipated, but not spiteful; and still other events entail malicious and spiteful intent. In classifying reasons for committing rule violations, Argyle et al. (1981) similarly suggest that some transgressions are deliberate (i.e., personal gain, trying to be funny), some "reflect inability on the part of the rule-breaker to recognise the applicability of the rule or to perform behaviors reflective of it," and some reflect "ignorance of the rule or of the conditions for its application" (p. 140). Whatever the actual responsibility, as a person's perceived linkage to an untoward act increases, so does the severity of the predicament for that person.

Chronic Susceptibility to Embarrassment

There are individual differences in the propensity to experience embarrassment across a diversity of face-threatening situations. Modigliani (1968) developed an instrument to measure this trait, which is called *embarrassability*. He found that the experience of embarrassment after a particular public failure is positively associated with embarrassability. Similarly, Miller (1987) found that subjects' embarrassability scores were significantly associated with the degree of personal embarrassment reported following the performance of an embarrassing task (e.g., imitating a child throwing a temper tantrum or singing "The Star-Spangled Banner"). In a survey of recalled embarrassing events, Miller (1992) also found a positive correlation between dispositional embarrassability and the intensity of embarrassment associated with the recalled event. Leary and Meadows (1991) have shown that the proclivity to blush is positively related to embarrassability as well. These data suggest that there are dispositional differences in people's concern for and sensitivity to face concerns (Cupach & Imahori, 1993a). "In general, people who dread disapproval from others and who especially desire to be liked and accepted tend to be uncommonly embarrassable as well as frequent blushers" (Miller & Leary, 1992, p. 207).

ᐓ Remedial Responses to Embarrassing Predicaments

Because embarrassing predicaments are face-threatening, people usually attempt to avoid performing embarrassing behaviors (Brown, 1970). However, when predicaments inevitably occur and embarrassment ensues, individuals are motivated to rectify the problematic situation and to *save* face (Goffman, 1967; Modigliani, 1971).

The experience of "embarrassment seems to have drive properties that promote attempts to repair threats to one's social image" (Miller & Leary, 1992). Facework employed to cope with embarrassing predicaments consists of remedial strategies (Cupach & Metts, 1990).

Remedial strategies accomplish multiple interrelated goals. By repairing damage to his or her own social identity, the embarrassed person counteracts the negative perceptions made by others (Cupach & Metts, 1990). This relieves some of the embarrassed person's psychological distress created by the predicament. In the long term, successfully coping with predicaments likely produces positive consequences for self-esteem and health (Snyder & Higgins, 1988, 1990; Weiner, Figueroa-Muñoz, & Kakihara, 1991). Remedial behavior also addresses the inconvenience, offensiveness, or harm perpetrated on others, whether unintentionally or deliberately. This compensates for the face loss that others have suffered, and thereby mitigates their anger and potentially aggressive retaliation (Ohbuchi, Kameda, & Agarie, 1989; Weiner, Amirkhan, Folkes, & Verette, 1987; Weiner & Handel, 1985; Yirmiya & Weiner, 1986). In reaffirming the identities of interactants, remedial behavior thwarts the escalation of interpersonal conflict (Schonbach, 1990) and restores stability and normality to the ongoing social interaction (Goffman, 1967).

Remedial strategies offered during a predicament parallel the facework behaviors outlined in Chapter 1 (apologies, accounts, avoidance, humor, remediation, and so on). In a study of recollected embarrassing situations, we identified the relative frequency with which embarrassed actors and observers utilize these various strategies (Metts & Cupach, 1989b); Table 2.1 shows these findings. The appropriateness, and hence selection, of any remedial action depends largely on the nature of the face-threatening event creating the predicament.

The Influence of Predicament Type on Remedial Strategies

Strategies employed to cope with embarrassing predicaments are tailored to the nature and degree of face loss attendant on the

Table 2.1 Remedial Strategies Utilized by Embarrassed Persons and
             Observers (in percentages)

Strategy	Embarrassed Person	Observer
Apology	11	1
Excuse	13	7
Justification	6	9
Humor	15	16
Remediation	17	5
Avoidance	34	12
Aggression	4	—
Empathy	—	19
Support	—	32

situation. Sharkey and Stafford (1990) asked respondents to recall
and describe three different embarrassing incidents: one in which
they were highly embarrassed, one in which they were moderately embarrassed, and one in which they experienced mild embarrassment. The researchers failed to discover differences in the
use of remedial strategies across the three levels of embarrassment
intensity. However, they did find differences in responses depending upon the cause of the embarrassment. For example, embarrassed persons responded to criticism from others most often with
hostility, whereas they responded to violations of privacy with
remediation (such as closing a door, buttoning a blouse).

In a study we conducted (Metts & Cupach, 1989b), we solicited
recollections of highly embarrassing incidents and classified them
into four general types (see Weinberg, 1968):

1. faux pas (misinterpreting a situation, such as wearing informal attire
   to a formal function)
2. accidents (unintentional awkward acts such as tripping or belching)
3. mistakes (performing ineptly, such as forgetting one's checkbook to
   pay for groceries)
4. recipient (being the victim of another's face-threatening act, such as
   being ridiculed by another or having one's privacy invaded by
   another)

Descriptive accounts of remedial strategies indicated that excuses were more likely to be offered in mistake situations, but less likely to be offered in recipient situations. Justifications were more likely in faux pas situations, whereas humor and remediation were more likely in accident situations. As would be expected, aggression was used by embarrassed individuals who were recipients of the face-threatening behavior of another, such as being teased, ridiculed, or criticized. This corresponds to results reported in other investigations (Cupach & Metts, 1992; Sharkey & Stafford, 1990).

In another study, we found that apologies were given by embarrassed individuals more frequently in situations of rule violations and failed role performance (Cupach & Metts, 1992). These types of incidents are more likely than other types (such as loss of comportment) to threaten the face of others and disrupt the social order. Hence relatively mitigating remedial moves directed at others are clearly appropriate. Accounts were more likely to be offered in situations of damaged self-image. Because these events call into question one's face, it is logical that accounts be used to redefine one's role in the predicament and the severity of event. Humor was more likely to appear in situations where a person lost comportment, but less likely when the person vicariously experienced the observed chagrin of another (i.e., empathic embarrassment).

Collectively, the research on remedial strategies indicates that some behaviors appear to be effectively face-saving across numerous contexts (i.e., apologies and remediation), whereas other strategies are more situationally limited in their utility (i.e., justifications). Cupach et al. (1986) explain:

> Both remediation and apology are indications of willingness to place one's own face needs second to the requirements for re-establishment of social order and second to the face needs of others. Remediation achieves this through implicit acknowledgment of responsibility without minimising the event and apology achieves this through explicit but unsolicited self-castigation. (pp. 196-197)

As we suggested in Chapter 1, contextual factors affect the placement of any remedial response on the aggravation-mitigation continuum. For example, the perceived credibility, sincerity, and character of a person offering a remedial response will affect the attributed level of aggravation or mitigation of the response. An excuse for tardiness from a chronic latecomer will be less mitigating than the very same excuse proffered by a first-time offender. Tedeschi (1990) explains that remedial behaviors that are "intended to protect identities, are themselves made more or less effective by the identities of the actor" (p. 319).

Second, remedial responses of a particular type are not necessarily equivalent in their consequences. Variations in the content of any particular remedial strategy will yield differences in evaluation of the remedial behavior (e.g., Hale, 1987). The nature of excuses and justifications can be quite variable; not all "excuses" are created equal. Research has yet to untangle the complexities of which types of excuses are more or less efficacious.

Third, the delivery of a remedial response—that is, the nonverbal characteristics—can substantially alter or modify the evaluative consequences of remedial messages. Two different apologies containing precisely the same verbal message will be interpreted differently depending upon how sarcastic, sincere, disingenuous, or repentant the apology "sounds."

Principles Guiding Effective Facework in Predicaments

Acknowledging a loss of face may be helpful, indeed sometimes necessary, for an individual to regain face effectively in an embarrassing predicament. Semin and Manstead (1982) elicited reactions from subjects who observed a shopper accidentally toppling a grocery store display. They found that the shopper who appeared to be embarrassed was rated more favorably by observers than the shopper who expressed no chagrin whatsoever. Other studies suggest that the appearance of embarrassment can elicit more positive evaluations from observers (Edelmann, 1982), engender greater efforts on the part of observers to offer assistance (Levin & Arluke, 1982), and possibly mitigate punishment for a transgression (Semin & Papadopoulou, 1990). The state of embarrassment is displayed through blushing, eye gaze aversion, nervous laughter, and the like. By showing the appearance of embarrassment, an individual accepts some responsibility for the event creating face loss and communicates regret or repentance (Castelfranchi & Poggi, 1990). Thus nonverbal displays of embarrassment may function in the same way as a simple verbal apology (Edelmann, 1987) or, in some cases, reinforce an apology by underscoring its sincerity.

Although the mere appearance of embarrassment can help to mitigate the negative repercussions of a face-threatening predicament, it is important that composure be regained and that the normal pattern of interaction be restored. Thus the display of poise is an important ingredient in saving face during predicaments. Goffman (1967) defines poise as "the capacity to suppress and conceal any tendency to become shamefaced during encounters with others" (p. 9). Poise in the face of a predicament demonstrates that the embarrassed person can regain composure and perform the repairs necessary to restore his or her social image. By assisting in the restoration of face subsequent to its loss, the embarrassed person "makes points" with fellow interactants. In part because such efforts demonstrate a form of social competence, the individual compensates for the temporary damage to image and thereby is worthy of regaining social approval. Humor is often effectively employed by embarrassed individuals who have behaved clumsily (Edelmann, 1985; Metts & Cupach, 1989b). The diminution or absence of poise reflects a loss of control and insufficient ability to cope with the events creating the problematic situation. Such a loss of control would threaten one's face even further—adding insult to injury.

Exhibiting poise is not merely for the sake of the embarrassed individual. An inability to recover smoothly from an embarrassing event will further disrupt the social interaction, and will undoubtedly exacerbate the predicament. Consequently, the embarrassed person becomes even more embarrassed about the inability to remedy the situation. This has the effect of making the other persons present experience embarrassment on behalf of the originally embarrassed person. Embarrassment is contagious (Goffman, 1967; Miller, 1987). If an embarrassed individual cannot make efforts to restore face loss on his or her own behalf, then it becomes more difficult for others to assist in repairing the predicament. Thus the faces of others are threatened on two counts: They are undermined in their ability to assist easily the embarrassed person in recovering from face loss, and they too have now lost face by becoming abashed over the increasingly chaotic encounter.

Whereas some embarrassing events primarily threaten the face of the person creating a predicament (e.g., tripping), other events directly threaten the face of other interactants. To spill a drink on oneself merely damages one's own social image. To spill a drink on another person embarrasses both the "spiller" and the "spilled on." As a predicament becomes increasingly face-threatening to others, the person responsible for the event is obligated to redress the face loss experienced by others if the responsible person's own face is to be restored. As predicaments become more severe, individuals experience greater negative repercussions and are more motivated to engage actively in remedial behavior (Schlenker, 1980). Moreover, observers expect remedial responses to be *legitimate*, that is, to be commensurate with the level of inconvenience or aggravation that accrues to them (Blumstein et al., 1974; Scott & Lyman, 1968). Consequently, as the severity of a predicament increases, ordinarily so does the mitigating nature of remedial responses. As a person's apparent responsibility for an act and the negative nature of an act increase, offending persons are more likely to offer concessions, more explicit and elaborate apologies, and apologies that are accompanied by accounts (Cupach & Metts, 1992; Fraser, 1981; Knapp et al., 1986; McLaughlin, Cody, & O'Hair, 1983; Schlenker & Darby, 1981). More elaborate apologies produce less blame, more forgiveness, more liking, perceptions of greater remorse, and sometimes less punishment (Darby & Schlenker, 1982, 1989). Ironically, when face threat accrues primarily to others, an offending person may have to undermine his or her own face to save the face of others. If others have been seriously affronted, the offending person may inflict self-punishment and thereby obviate the need for others to administer sanctions.

As we shall discover in subsequent chapters, to threaten a relational partner's face, particularly in a close relationship, is virtually to threaten the relationship itself. Consequently, as the seriousness of face threat to a partner increases, and as the intimacy of the relationship increases, there will be greater pressure to redress the partner's face loss. The offending partner must be responsive to both the personal and relational implications of committing the face threat (Fincham, 1992). In later chapters we will discuss more serious face-threatening events, such as relational transgressions. For now, we turn to a brief discussion regarding the functioning of embarrassing predicaments in close relationships.

❧ Embarrassment in Close Relationships

Given that embarrassment is aversive and face-threatening, it is logical to assume that happy relational partners generally avoid embarrassing each other. Petronio, Olson, and Dollar (1988) attempted to verify that being embarrassed by a close relational partner would be problematic for the relationship. Respondents were asked to describe embarrassing situations caused by their romantic partners. Content analysis revealed three primary types of relational embarrassment: revealing relational secrets, inappropriate actions, and awkward situations. Examples of these situations are given in Table 2.2. The authors inferred from these categories that relational embarrassment primarily involves violation of expectations regarding relational privacy issues.

Petronio et al. asked their respondents why their partners had caused embarrassment and found six categories of reasons: done unintentionally (37%), trying to be humorous (13%), attempting to control the relationship (17%), impressing others at the partner's expense (15%), violating a norm intentionally (11%), and retaliating (8%). In a separate study, Sharkey (1991) found that individuals reported a number of explicit goals for *intentionally* embarrassing other persons, including to show solidarity, to negatively sanction unwanted behavior, to exercise power, to discredit another, and to obtain self-gratification. Clearly, these two investigations demonstrate that embarrassment is not always unanticipated and accidental. Sometimes it is deliberately perpetrated by one relational partner

Table 2.2 Embarrassing Relational Situations

Revealing relational secrets
    Revealing sexual behaviors between partners
    Revealing past private experiences
    Revealing intimate feelings shared between partners
    Revealing relational problems in public
    Revealing a concealed relationship
    Revealing negative feelings about the partner

Inappropriate actions
    Explicit sexual advances in public
    Verbal/physical abuse
    Openly flirting with others in front of partner
    Intentional inattentiveness to romantic partner
    Frequent interruptions
    Talking lovingly about prior relationship in front of others

Awkward situations
    Partner makes scene in public while other is watching
    Partner acts inappropriately

SOURCE: Petronio et al. (1988). Reprinted by permission of the authors.

on another. Moreover, the motives behind such intentional embarrassment range from constructive to destructive.

Petronio et al. also asked respondents to assess the effect of *frequency* of embarrassment on feelings regarding relational satisfaction and relational communication. Results indicated that current relationships exhibited greater longevity, exhibited less embarrassment, and produced higher ratings of relational quality and relational communication satisfaction compared with terminated relationships. It is likely, however, that the purpose and type of created embarrassment, as well as the manner in which it is remedied, exert greater effects on relational outcomes than does sheer frequency of embarrassment.

Sharkey (1993) examined relational differences in the use of *intentional* embarrassment. He surveyed individuals about events in which each had intentionally embarrassed another. A wide range of relationships between embarrassor and the embarrassed party were included in the sample: intimate partners, friends and extended family, parents and in-laws, sons and daughters, superiors and subordinates, siblings, and strangers. However, friends and intimate partners were cited as recipients of the intentionally embarrassing behavior in about 75% of the cases. Moreover, the most frequently cited goal for creating intentional embarrassment was *to foster solidarity*. Thus embarrassment may play a positive role in relationships, perhaps serving as a form of relational play (Baxter, 1992) that functions to create and sustain intimacy.

Sharkey (1993) asserts that the presence of intentional embarrassment in close relationships may reflect the fact that protecting a partner's face is less important as relationships become more intimate. Face maintenance is always important, however. More likely, what is perceived as face-threatening changes over the course of a relationship, and relationships that have developed stability and interdependence can withstand greater amounts of face threat. In Petronio's sample, it seems likely that those respondents reporting on past relationships recalled embarrassing incidents that were face-threatening (whether performed intentionally or unintentionally). Recalling such events may be consistent with the memory of a relationship where a number of things were problematic. Further, there is evidence that the relative frequency of embarrassing events overall is lower in intimate relationships (Sharkey & Stafford, 1988). This is probably because unintentional embarrassment is less likely given the familiarity that has developed between partners. Faux pas, for example, are less likely to occur and are less likely to be embarrassing in intimate relationships (Harris, 1984; Knapp et al., 1986). Intentional embarrassment may be more likely in intimate relationships, and its use can be constructive or destructive with respect to the relationship.

⋞ Summary

Embarrassing predicaments occur when there is a discrepancy between the image that a person wishes to portray and the image that is actually presented during social interaction. Because a person's image is manifested concretely through face, facework is the mechanism by which individuals repair the damage done and restore the desired self-image. Social situations that lead to embarrassment constitute the prototypical context for studying face loss and face repair.

Embarrassment can occur in the context of any social or personal relationship, but as relationships become more intimate, the complexion of face concerns gets more complicated. In Chapter 3, we delineate how face is implicated in the development of a close relationship. Specifically, we consider how face issues arise as partners manage the escalation of informational and physical intimacy.

3

Managing Vulnerability in Escalating Relationships

I sometimes "play dumb" on dates, but it leaves a bad taste. The emotions are complicated. Part of me enjoys "putting something over" on the unsuspecting male. But this sense of superiority over him is mixed with feelings of guilt for my hypocrisy. Toward the "date" I feel some contempt because he is "taken in" by my technique, or if I like the boy, a kind of maternal condescension. At times I resent him! Why isn't he my superior in all ways in which a man should excel so that I could be my natural self?

And the funny part of it is that the man, I think, is not always so unsuspecting. He may sense the truth and become uneasy in the relation. "Where do I stand? Is she laughing up her sleeve or did she mean this praise? Was she really impressed with that little speech of mine or did she only pretend to know nothing about politics?" And once or twice I felt that the joke was on me; the boy saw through my wiles and felt contempt for me for stooping to such tricks. (Komarovsky, as cited by Goffman, 1959, pp. 236-237)

Face is a very important component in the difficult process of creating a close relationship. As the above quote illustrates, we often construct faces or personas that actually lead away from our "natural" selves because we think we should display certain characteristics. We have internalized some implicit set of rules or instructions that tell us X identity or Y identity would be appropriate in a certain circumstance. The college student who provided the example above internalized a belief that she should not appear to be smarter than her date—a belief that led her away from more genuine personas. In a similar fashion, some college men may have internalized beliefs that they should be strong, athletic, logical, nonemotional, and so forth. In fact, a substantial part of forming a relationship is learning which elements of the identity presented in public are constant across situations and which are present only during certain types of situations. Those that are more generalized are probably more central to a person's "natural" self.

Of course, we can present any identity (or maintain a face) only to the extent that it is supported by the other people present during the interaction. Part of what we find initially attractive about a person is his or her ability or inclination to support an identity that is comfortable or satisfying to us. This person makes both our proposed identity and our performance of that identity seem valued. Likewise, he or she presents an identity that we find easy to support. Part of the relationship development process is risking exposure of private elements of the self that we fear may adversely affect a partner's impression of us. This chapter examines three areas of intimacy: getting acquainted, initiating sexual involvement, and developing symbolic interdependence. These constitute areas where people are particularly vulnerable to a potential partner's rejection.

ꙮ Social Face Becomes Relationship-Specific Face

At the close of Chapter 2, we offered a brief discussion of how intimacy allows a couple to adapt social structures and processes to their own circumstances. Although intentional face threat is not expected in most social situations, we often find it in the form of teasing and play in close relationships (Baxter, 1992; Betcher, 1981). Does this mean that intimates do not respect the face needs of their partners? Quite the contrary—respect for face needs is fundamental to all healthy relationships.

A better explanation is simply that a partner's "social face" is one type of persona, and it is seldom the prominent persona during a couple's ordinary interactions. Thus arriving late to a meeting with one's spouse or teasing a friend about being "asexual" or "sexually perverted" is not usually a threat to face in the strict sense because social competence is presumed or taken for granted. With a relative stranger, however, these same behaviors are very face-threatening, because there is no interpretive framework: Late arrival devalues the other person's time and indicates potential lack of punctuality in the late arriver, and sexual jokes call into question another person's sexual competence or integrity. The liberties we sometimes take in asking special favors of a partner or arriving at a meeting late, or dressing casually, or teasing each other about eating too much or eating too fast are all ways of expressing the fact that social performance and relationship-specific performance have different expectations and are judged by different standards.

As a way to explain this difference, Goffman (1959) uses a dramatistic metaphor; that is, he draws an analogy between social interaction and a play. Accordingly, he says, people have a backstage and frontstage in which they operate. The frontstage is the "playing area," where we do our performance. As Goffman (1959) explains about performance, it is the mechanism by which we construct a "self" for a particular situation that has the traits and qualities we deem most appropriate for that situation. Other people who are present in the situation act as an audience and thereby support our performance. But we also have a backstage area, where we prepare ourselves for performance. For most of us, this area is our home; it may also exist in such places as a bus ride to work during which we rehearse possible scenarios for the day. For college professors and other people whose competence is judged by how they perform as teachers and writers, the backstage area might also be an office or a study. In this example, when a teacher moves from the office where he or she has been working on a lecture to the classroom where students sit as the audience, he or she enters frontstage and begins the performance.

As a relationship develops from a somewhat formal and casual relationship into an intimate one, the individuals involved begin to share more and more of the backstage area. Both physically and psychologically they "let each other in" and remove the "constructed" identities that mark frontstage performance. Of course, in so doing, each begins to reveal points of demarcation between his or her social persona and private persona—or, more accurately, private personas. One or the other may, in fact, decide that he or she likes the social persona he or she met initially more than the private personas and may curtail development of the relationship. On the other hand, he or she may find that the other's private and public personas are not much different or are at least complementary. Assuming these personas are attractive and give support to a persona that the other person wants to put forth, he or she will continue developing the relationship.

If a relationship develops toward greater intimacy, backstage behavior, even when not physically in a backstage setting, begins to appear in the couple's interactions. Thus they become more blunt, less guarded, more critical, and so forth. Mark Knapp and Anita Vangelisti (1992) capture the essence of this shift in one of the eight dimensions of communication that change as a couple moves toward intimacy. They say that in addition to changes in such dimensions as ritualized to spontaneous communication and stylized to unique communication, a couple's communication moves along a continuum they label "overt judgment suspended to overt judgment given." In early phases of relationships, evaluative comments such as "I wish you would work out" or "I wish you didn't arrive late all the time" are thought, but not stated. Eventually, they are voiced and "overt judgment" is given. This is an important change in the communication pattern of a couple; it means that they feel the relationship is personalized enough to act as a

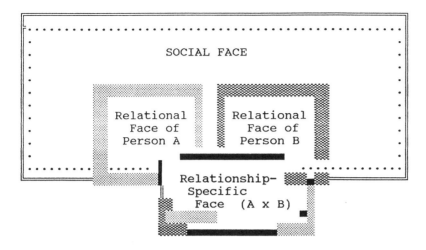

Figure 3.1. The Embeddedness of Social, Relational, and Relationship-Specific Aspects of Face

buffer or framework to contextualize criticism. Thus a couple can give and take criticism without loss of face as they might experience it in a "social" or "public" context.

Figure 3.1 depicts the various points we have raised so far and helps elaborate them in more detail. The broadest concept is *social face*. It is the identity that we perform in most daily interactions with role-related individuals and nonintimates. *Relational face* is the face that people assume will be appropriate to contexts that are quasi-relational or potentially relational, but that do not involve one's actual relational partner. For example, the college student who described her feelings of frustration at "playing dumb" was expressing her awareness that "how-I-will-be" relative to another person is influenced by the context. She wonders why a man cannot simply be her "superior" in the ways in which a "man should excel" so that she can be her natural self. But she clearly does not mean a "natural self" in other contexts, for example, a job interview. She would never say, "Sometimes at a job interview I play dumb."

The smallest area in Figure 3.1 is called *relationship-specific face* because it is the face we present to a particular other person—friend or family, spouse or other romantic partner—in the context of that relationship. It contains elements of social face and elements of relational face. But it is also adapted uniquely for each couple. This is why some couples say that they never argue, and yet children and neighbors would say they argue all of the time. In essence, both views are accurate. For the couple, disagreement over ideas might not be considered arguing; only disagreement over relational definition or functions would be considered arguing. Onlookers who hear them arguing over ideas are working with the social or relational interpretive frames, whereas the couple is working within their own relationship-specific frame. Similarly, many relationship-specific frames incorporate the more general relational trait of sexual fidelity, but some do not. This is why discussions of relationship deception and relationship transgressions need to take account of the uniqueness of relationship definitions.

Another way to characterize the relationship-specific face we have been discussing is to use the concept of relationship "culture." Culture in a general sense is a set of attitudes, values, and beliefs that tell people how to act and how to interpret the behavior of other people. It provides its members with rules and scripts for appropriate conduct in particular contexts. This level of culture is therefore comparable to our level of social face.

But as relationships develop, these broad and undifferentiated guidelines are not adequate for the day-to-day interactions and unique circumstances of a couple. Even generalized rules and expectations about how to "do relationships" that we would place at the second level of our diagram are not adequate. In order to do their particular relationship with its particular features and limitations, the couple co-constructs a culture of their own that provides them with a shared understanding of what will be the attitudes, beliefs, values, rules, and appropriate behaviors that will define their relationship. As Julia Wood (1982) explains:

> To carve an identity within a particular relationship is to become a
> substantially different self than the one existing prior to the relation-

ship. As a relationship becomes more intimate and a partner more significant, an individual's self-definition increasingly takes into account the understandings of the evolving relational culture. (p. 77)

Thus each individual's personal identity is affected by involvement in the relationship. At the same time, the developing relationship represents the merging and interconnection of the identities of the individual relational partners. The processes by which individuals explore the possibilities of such a merger are reflected in attempts to reduce uncertainty and seek affinity. We now turn to these processes.

⁊ Getting Acquainted

Development of a relationship-specific culture is an interesting phenomenon. Have you ever talked with a friend or romantic partner about the beginning of your relationship? Can you trace it back to the first meeting? Was it in elementary school? Junior high school? High school? Does it seem like you have known this person forever? Or is it the case that you met at college, at work, or through a friend? Do you laugh now about the initial awkwardness, the misperceptions, the confusions over exactly what the relationship was going to become? Researchers have been studying relationship development for some time. Their research findings help us answer the question of how people meet and co-construct a relationship-specific culture without threatening face.

How is it that getting to know another person can threaten face? There are two primary ways, which we consider here: fear of rejection and fear of imposition. Whenever we ask a potential partner out on a date or ask a potential friend to join us in an activity, we risk rejection. This is threat to positive face. Whenever the other person feels compelled to go, or has to adjust his or her schedule, or feels obligated to go, that person has experienced threat to negative face. In order to minimize the occurrence of either type of threat, people use certain tactics to assess the situation in indirect ways. This indirectness allows them to learn information that will help them avoid possible rejection and imposition and to do so in a way that doesn't threaten the other person's privacy in the process. In addition, when people engage in conversation, they try to establish a sense of commonality and trust that will minimize any face threats that do arise. These concerns lead us to present two areas of relevant research: uncertainty reduction and affinity seeking.

Uncertainty Reduction

Several years ago, Charles Berger and Richard Calabrese (1975) proposed a theory of information acquisition called *uncertainty reduction theory*. Basically, this theory says that during initial interactions, our lack of knowledge about another person causes us to be uneasy or uncomfortable. We therefore set about to find ways to reduce this uncertainty. Asking questions is clearly one way to reduce uncertainty, but this is actually a last resort, because questions are face-threatening to the person being questioned. They put the other person in the position of having to answer, because not answering a direct question makes a person appear rude. Readers who have ever found themselves engaging in "white lies" with a new acquaintance because he or she kept asking questions they didn't want to answer recognize the "have-to-answer" nature of questions. If people don't ask, one can simply avoid the topic. In initial interactions, therefore, people usually counterbalance their need to obtain information efficiently with the needs to be socially appropriate and to protect face (Douglas, 1987).

If we use techniques that are less threatening to face than questions, what might they be? Berger and his colleagues suggest that there are three general categories of techniques that people use to reduce uncertainty; they label these passive, active, and interactive (see, e.g., Berger, 1979; Berger & Bradac, 1982). *Passive* strategies include the numerous ways we gather information about other persons from behind the scenes. One such strategy might be to observe a person in unstructured social situations to see how he or she acts when situations are ambiguous and emergent. *Active* strategies include such devices as asking people in the social network about a target person and structuring a social episode to see how a target person responds. For example, if one has been watching an attractive person at a party, one might get a friend to ask him or her to dance in order to gauge the reaction. If the person seems willing to dance, at least one can infer that he or she is sociable and possibly unattached. *Interactive* strategies are used when the seeker and the target are actually engaged in conversation. These are the most direct and therefore the most threatening, for both the seeker and the target. Two common techniques in this category are self-disclosure and interrogatives (questions). Self-disclosure works to reduce uncertainty because there is such a strong norm of reciprocity. If one person discloses a little, the other person usually matches this investment. And finally, as we noted above, people can simply jump in feet first and ask questions: "So, are you dating or engaged or anything like that? Do ya wanna date?"

Affinity Seeking

During social interaction, individuals communicate in ways that are designed to get other people to like and feel positive toward them. In the terms we are using in this book, they attempt to establish early on a sense of support for the positive face of the other and to elicit regard for their own positive face. Bell and Daly (1984) delineate the various ways in which interactants cultivate interpersonal attraction by communicating and seeking affinity (i.e., commonality, mutuality, regard, and so on). Some of the strategies include (a) presenting oneself as trustable and trusting, (b) being polite, (c) expressing concern and care for the other, (d) signaling interest in the other and fostering his or her conversational involvement, and (e) stressing commonalities and similarities. Research conducted by Bell and Daly (1984) has confirmed that the use of affinity-seeking strategies is positively associated with interpersonal attraction, social effectiveness, and life satisfaction.

To summarize, the research on initial interactions suggests that people are more indirect than direct in how they come to learn about others. People are also attentive to their own face needs and those of others. We would never want to say that violating these normative patterns will prevent the development of a relationship. It is not uncommon to hear a person say to his or her romantic partner, "I don't know how I ever fell in love with you; I thought you were such a jerk when we first met." However, if social structures do not bring two people into contact on a regular basis, the quality of the initial meeting usually will determine whether or not effort is made to meet again.

Reducing uncertainty and cultivating affinity are intrinsic to the process of developing *psychological* intimacy. But physical attraction often sparks the initiation of intimate relationships. Thus couples must also manage the escalation of *physical* intimacy.

❧ Negotiating Sexual Involvement

Managing issues of sexuality in relationships is tricky. The subject of sex can be awkward, and situations involving the negotiation of sexual involvement are potentially very face-threatening. For a number of reasons, people find it difficult to talk explicitly about their sexual needs and desires with their relational partners, especially prior to the development of a sexual relationship. "A sexual episode presents individuals with an extraordinary situation that is arguably more vulnerable and volatile than almost any other interaction context" (Edgar & Fitzpatrick, 1990, p. 107). Even some spouses who have had intercourse hundreds of times find it extremely difficult to discuss sexual matters with each other.

Aside from the fact that we are socialized to believe that sex talk is taboo, it is also the case that sex talk is emotionally dangerous. Sex talk involves disclosure that has implications for how one's identity is judged (e.g., frigid, promiscuous, aggressive, deviant). It is therefore acutely associated with the face-threatening feelings of shame, guilt, and embarrassment (Metts & Cupach, 1989a). Myron Brenton (1973) describes how expressing our feelings about sex makes us particularly vulnerable:

> It's emotional talk not only because of guilt but also because of risk. To verbalize anything is to expose it, transform it from something

private into something public. Once it's public it's open to judgment, to criticism. More precisely, when we're open with respect to
our sexual feelings and wishes, *we're* open to judgment, to criticisms,
to put-downs, to rejection. (p. 21)

Because sexual situations are so emotionally charged, the need to
save face in them is particularly acute (Edgar & Fitzpatrick, 1990).

Moreover, talking about sex (as opposed to talking sexy) seems
to take some of the "steam" out of actually having sex. Part of the
excitement and arousal associated with sexual activity stems from
its atmosphere of mystery and uncertainty (Adelman, 1992). For
these reasons, sexual encounters in relationships are negotiated
tacitly and abstractly. There are numerous issues that partners
must coordinate in order for a sexual relationship to be satisfying.
We will focus on the relatively obvious aspects of initiating and
refusing intercourse and negotiating the practice of safe sex.

Sexual Initiation

The attempt to initiate sexual activity in a relationship is usually
accomplished by indirect means (e.g., McCormick, 1979). Hinting,
nonverbal posturing, and verbal innuendo are typically used to
indicate sexual interest and to test the waters. The traditional
"script" for sexual activity in our culture holds that men initiate
sexual activity, whereas women control whether and "how far"
sexual activity will go (LaPlante, McCormick, & Brannigan, 1980;
Peplau, Rubin, & Hill, 1977). Given the indirectness and ambiguity surrounding flirtation and presexual behavior, however, it may
be difficult to discern who really initiates a sexual encounter.
Women may engage in "proceptive" behaviors such as extended
eye gaze or increased touching to signal that they are open to
sexual advances (Moore, 1985; Perper & Weis, 1987). The same
behaviors, however, may be intended to draw a potential partner's attention, to communicate liking, or to express relational
(but not necessarily sexual) interest.

Indirectness in the initiation of sexual activity avoids face loss
for the initiator in the event that the partner does not wish to
comply with the initiator's goal of having sex. Because an explicit

request was not made, the partner does not have to refuse bla-
tantly and the initiator is not overtly rejected (Cupach & Metts,
1991). Also, the indirect initiation respects the negative face of the
partner by being less imposing than a direct request, and by not
putting the partner in the awkward or embarrassing position of
having to reject (and possibly embarrass) the initiator.

In developed sexual relationships, such as marriage or cohabi-
tation, couples may abandon the cultural norms for initiating sex
and develop their own idiosyncratic dyadic scripts. The development of a relational culture allows the couple to negotiate what
they think is appropriate and comfortable behavior. Partners become more concerned with relationship-specific face than with
social face. Wives, for example, tend to be more comfortable in
initiating intercourse (Brown & Auerback, 1981). It can be argued
that:

> some of a woman's reluctance to initiate sex during courtship is
> based on the need to keep herself marketable within the persistent
> confines of the sexual double standard. Thus, once the formal rela-
> tionship commitment is made, she can assume that her sexual ad-
> vances are evaluated as a positive attribute of the relationship (i.e.,
> love) rather than a potentially negative attribute of her personality
> (i.e., promiscuity). (Cupach & Metts, 1991, p. 101)

In short, the social norms that govern the early negotiation of
sexual behavior become displaced by the norms attendant on the
mutually negotiated relational culture.

Initiation of sexual behavior in close relationships with a sexual
history still tends to be nonverbal and somewhat indirect (Brown
& Auerback, 1981; Byers & Heinlein, 1989), though the intent is
probably less ambiguous to relational partners. Because partners
gain familiarity with the meaning of each other's behavior, they
are better able to interpret cues and manage potential face threat
more effectively. For example, a husband may be able to predict
his chances for success by testing the climate with proceptive cues.
If his wife is unresponsive to the subtle overture, he may postpone
his initiation of sexual behavior until a more promising opportunity is available. Similarly, if the husband senses that his wife is

interested in having sex, but he is not in the mood, he can make himself "unavailable" so that his wife does not have sufficient opportunity to initiate a sexual encounter. Without the opportunity for initiation, there is no need to resist actively.

Sexual Resistance

Because initiation of sexual activity is ambiguous, particularly when a sexual component has not yet been established in the relationship, it leaves open to question the motives and goals of the initiator. Does the presexual behavior signal an interest in advancing the emotional intimacy of the relationship? Or does it indicate the initiator's desire for having intercourse? Or perhaps a combination of both? Or perhaps the person is simply exceptionally friendly with all acquaintances? The decision to comply or not with a perceived sexual overture may very well depend on the motives ascribed to the initiator.

When the initiation of sexual activity is ambiguous, it is risky in terms of face threat to resist too overtly. The initiator, upon being embarrassed, could deny the attributed intent to initiate sex, making the resistor look bad. However, it is also risky to be too ambiguous because the resistor may fail to communicate effectively that sexual activity is unwanted. Thus resistance messages must be clear enough to resist initiation effectively, but also sensitive enough to save face (Metts, Cupach, & Imahori, 1992).

The ambiguity surrounding the negotiation of sexual activity is complicated by a number of factors. First, men and women seem to have different thresholds for perceiving the sexual intent of another (Shotland & Craig, 1988). Men are more inclined than women to interpret friendly social behavior in a sexual manner (Abbey, 1982; Abbey & Melby, 1986; Muehlenhard & Linton, 1987). Second, men perceive that women offer "token" resistance so as not to appear overly eager and promiscuous. Indeed, there is evidence that some women show resistance to a sexual advance when they actually intend to have sex. One survey of college women indicated that 40% had engaged in token resistance on at least one occasion (Muehlenhard & Hollabaugh, 1988). Third, women, who by virtue of the cultural script are usually in the role of recipient (rather than initiator) of a sexual advance, tend to be more polite and indirect (i.e., face-saving) than men in situations of compliance (e.g., Baxter, 1984; Falbo & Peplau, 1980). Not surprisingly, however, direct and persistent verbal or physical responses are more effective in preventing unwanted sex (Byers, 1988; Christopher & Frandsen, 1990; Murnen, Perot, & Byrne, 1989).

Practicing Safe Sex

When sexual activity is being planned, there are usually multiple goals being managed by partners. In spite of the risks of pregnancy and sexually transmitted diseases, including AIDS, partners are sometimes reluctant to broach the subject of practicing safe sex. Edgar and Fitzpatrick (1988) identify several reasons persons might fail to engage in safe-sex behaviors: lack of skills, fear of homosexual association, reluctance to bring it up because it might destroy the erotic mood, and lack of personalization of risk. Bringing up the subject of safe sex might also entail the risk of being labeled presumptuous or, worse, promiscuous. There seems to be an inherent incongruity between the rational, pragmatic, and strategic considerations of safe-sex talk and the erotic, passionate, and spontaneous characteristics associated with sexual arousal (e.g., Adelman, 1991, 1992).

Embarrassment is common in sexual encounters, and is often sufficient to deter a person from requesting that a male sexual partner wear a condom. One recent study found that the most frequently cited reason for not discussing AIDS with a relational partner was the fear of embarrassment—both one's own and the partner's (Cline, Johnson, & Freeman, 1992). Thus the fear of face threat sometimes supersedes rather significant health concerns. Christa Arnold and Jane Honska (1992; Honska & Arnold, 1992) have identified eight strategies for reducing embarrassment in sexual situations. By reducing embarrassment, these strategies have the potential to facilitate condom use. Table 3.1 gives examples of each strategy.

In their research, Arnold and Honska (1992) found that the *relational* strategy was perceived by both men and women to reduce

Table 3.1 Embarrassment Reduction Strategies in Sexual Situations

Acknowledgment	verbally recognizing that the partner is embarrassed (e.g., "I know this is embarrassing.")
Action	proceeding with sexual foreplay or putting on the condom (e.g., "I would attempt to help my date feel more sensual by increasing foreplay" or "I would just take the condom and put it on.")
Denial	refusing to allow the other person to be embarrassed (e.g., "Don't be embarrassed.")
Humor	joking or trying to have fun with the situation (e.g., "I'd try to make light of the situation—make a joke—like, 'Junior's got to put on his raincoat.'")
Inquiry	questioning or asking about feelings (e.g., "I'd ask what she/he thought about using a condom and see what was said" or "What's wrong? Does this bother you?")
Rationale	giving reasons for using a condom (e.g., "Better safe than sorry.")
Relational	showing concern for the relationship and/or the partner (e.g., "Comfort her/him and show that what I'm doing is best for the both of us.")
Ultimatum	demanding that a condom be used or there will be no sexual intercourse (e.g., "No condom, no sex!")

SOURCE: Arnold and Honska (1992). Reprinted by permission of the authors.

embarrassment most effectively. Apparently, showing a concern for the relationship is consistent with the degree of intimacy associated with sexual involvement. Interestingly, the number of sexual partners people had during the past year was associated with the strategies they were likely to employ. Those who reported having multiple partners during the past year tended to use the strategies of humor and action. These strategies appear to be adaptable to a variety of sexual partners.

As relationships develop sexual histories, partners alter the ways in which they manage the issue of safe sex. Couples who practice safe sex in the early phases of their relationships often abandon the practice as time goes by and/or expressed commitment occurs. This happens in spite of knowledge that AIDS symptoms take a long time to emerge, and that a significant percentage of relationally committed individuals engage in extradyadic (e.g., extramarital) sex. Ironically, the comfort and security afforded by the development of a relational culture simultaneously engenders personal risk. In the following section, we examine how individuals co-construct their relational cultures.

❧ Developing Symbolic Interdependence

Individuals who manage to develop intimate relationships do not merely come to know one another (in either or both the psychological and biblical senses). After all, familiarity does breed contempt—sometimes. Along with increased knowledge and physical contact, close relationships also develop increased solidarity and interdependence. These features are accomplished via the negotiation of a mutually shared relational culture, characterized by the merging of individual identities.

Prior to developing a relationship, individuals possess distinct and unconnected personal identities. Each person's identity is his or her self-conception, which serves as an interpretive frame for understanding social relationships as well as a source of personal motivations and expectations for social behavior. As individuals develop a relationship, they influence the makeup of each other's personal identity and create a shared aspect of each other's identity in the form of relational culture.

Part of a person's identity is his or her orientation to relationships. Individuals differ with respect to the beliefs and values they hold about close relationships in general. Garth Fletcher and Leah Kininmonth (1992) have developed a set of items representing various beliefs about what makes close relationships successful; some of these are listed below. Individuals differ in terms of the extent to which they hold these various beliefs.

"It is essential for partners to express all their feelings in relationships."
"Each partner has a right to absolute privacy."
"The best relationships are built on strong sexual attraction."

"Partners must be best friends as well as lovers."

"Courtesy toward the partner is one of the most important factors in the success of the best relationships."

Timothy Stephen and Howard Markman (1983; Stephen, 1986) have developed a similar set of items designed to measure intimacy orientations, called the Relational World Index. Some of the statements in the index include the following:

"A relationship should not be possessive or exclusive."

"Sex is not important to a relationship."

"In a good relationship, the partners manage to stay just a little bit mysterious to each other."

"Relationships should be oriented toward fun."

"Both partners should contribute equally to the relationship."

The manifestation of such beliefs represents an individual's relationship face. But these kinds of beliefs are not the sort of thing that individuals sit down and discuss openly early in the development of a relationship. Such beliefs are tacitly revealed over time through relationship behavior.

The sharing of relationship beliefs, and hence relationship faces, is integral to the development of relationship culture and hence relationship-specific face between partners. But how do the beliefs come to be shared? One way is that individuals may already have similar orientations when they meet; that is, they possess many of the same relationship beliefs. Over time, partners discover this similarity and reinforce it in their relationship behavior. It could be argued that similarity in relationship beliefs *predisposes* some individuals to develop compatible relationships.

The notion that similarity leads to interpersonal attraction is not new (Byrne, 1971). Historically, similarity has been seen as leading to attraction because sharing a relationship with a similar other is cognitively reinforcing. But we also believe that similarity facilitates relationship development because it fosters enjoyable interactions (Burleson & Denton, 1992) and catalyzes the development of relationship culture.

But close relationships do not survive only if partners by chance happen to share relationship beliefs when they first meet. As a relationship escalates and partners interact, they influence each other as they develop a relational culture. Thus, to some extent, the process of developing intimacy in close relationships entails the subtle development over time of an increasingly shared orientation about relationships. As the two relationship orientations exhibit overlap, relationship culture and relationship-specific face are formed.

Empirical research supports the claim that compatibility between partners with respect to relationship beliefs affects the viability of close relationships. Fletcher and Kininmonth (1992) found that relationship beliefs moderated the association between behaviors reported in relationships, and relationship satisfaction. Thus, for example, if an individual believes strongly that passion is important for a close relationship, then passionate behaviors in the relationship predict satisfaction. If an individual does not endorse this belief, then passionate behaviors are not predictive of satisfaction.

Research by Stephen also supports the phenomenon of developing relationship culture. He argues that the negotiated shared view of reality creates symbolic interdependence in relationships. Symbolic interdependence represents the correlation between two partners' orientations to relationships. Stephen's (1984a) research indicates that symbolic interdependence (a) is greater in actual couples compared with randomly matched persons, (b) is greater as relationships become more advanced, and (c) is positively associated with levels of relationship satisfaction and commitment. Higher degrees of symbolic interdependence are also associated with a lower likelihood of relational termination (Stephen, 1984b).

✿ Summary

Our goal in this chapter has been to identify some of the processes involved in the initiation and escalation of close relationships. Practices designed to reduce uncertainty and enhance affinity are characteristic of relationship development. These practices are necessarily constrained by concerns for face. Face threat is particularly acute during the initiation of sexual behavior in a relationship. Developing sexual intimacy is really a microcosm of the more general process of escalating closeness in a relationship. The development of close relationships entails balancing the need to protect face with the instrumental goal of advancing physical intimacy. To the extent these challenges are managed satisfactorily, individuals become a couple and share a relational culture.

Relational culture (and relationship-specific face) are not static states. Even in the most intimate and satisfying of relationships, partners encounter and must manage problematic episodes that can threaten the relational bond. In Chapter 4 we explore the dynamics of dealing with these inevitable relationship challenges.

4

Managing Problematic Episodes in Established Relationships

The focus of Chapter 3 was on the process by which individuals negotiate and co-construct their respective relationship-specific identities. Unfortunately, constructing these identities is only the beginning. As circumstances change, identities evolve. New challenges may require new rules. Expectations that once functioned adequately no longer suffice. In short, relationships will not be sustained at a very satisfying level for partners if they are not able to adapt to changing circumstances. This chapter examines three types of predicaments or problematic episodes that couples encounter over the course of a relationship. Each predicament arises from changing circumstances, and each potentially triggers change in the relationship culture. Obviously, change can be functional for the long-term duration of a relationship or it can be dysfunctional. Change can even be drastic enough to cause a couple to abandon all repair efforts and decide to terminate the relationship. Accomplishing the particular goal of relational dissolution from a face perspective is discussed in Chapter 5.

Three types of problematic situations can be illuminated from a face perspective. The first type of episode involves dealing with complaints and certain types of conflict that call into question the positive face of one's partner. The second problematic episode type concerns social support. In some ways this is the obverse of the complaint episode. Rather than calling into question the positive face of the recipient, the social support episode threatens the negative face of the support provider because his or her efforts to bolster the morale and esteem of the recipient are an imposition on time and emotional energy. Of course, partners willingly undertake reciprocal support on a regular basis. But requests for continuous social support for a romantic partner, friend, or family member who seems never to become emotionally stronger is eventually resented precisely because it drains the provider's negative face tolerance.

The third type of problematic episode is the most traumatic of the three because it involves the revelation and management of a relational transgression. It is impossible to say which type of face is most sorely implicated by a relational transgression. Serious transgressions, in fact, rock the very foundation of the relationship culture—the collection of rules, values, attitudes, and beliefs from which the relationship-specific identity is derived. Lesser transgressions may simply cause the couple to reevaluate the rules of their relationship or to reassess the meanings they ascribe to certain behaviors. In any event, all transgression episodes are difficult to manage because they implicate face at some level, either because a violation of face needs constitutes a violation of a fundamental rule of the relationship or because a violation of a rule threatens a partner's relationship-specific face.

✥ Complaints and Disagreements

Complaint episodes are problematic interactions because complaints are not generally about a person's social behavior, but about his or her relationship-specific behavior. Even though the behavior may have been done in public, the complaint is based on the perception by the complaining partner that the behavior causes a problem in the relationship. What is particularly difficult about complaint episodes for couples to manage is that not only is the process of complaining inherently face-threatening, but the topic of the complaint is often about face violations. Thus it is no surprise that complaint episodes often escalate into conflict when the recipient of the complaint reacts by attacking the face of the complainer. Jess Alberts and Gillian Driscoll (1992) offer a vivid illustration of this type of escalation within the taped conversation of two college students who are dating:

M: You often conclude my response to a situation without asking my opinion. For example, if I pick you up from work you think I will hold it against you in some way. I have told you that I don't mind doing you favors. However, you continue to do this and it has become quite irritating.

F: Okay, it's a problem that I . . . STOP IT! It's a problem that I conclude the answers? Or is it that you pick me up from work?

M: That you conclude my answers, Cindy. I said when I picked you up that was an example. An example.

F: Okay.

M: Would you say that you do that quite often?

F: Well

M: Did you know that it annoys me?

F: Charles, half the time you don't answer me 'cause you're tired or something. And I just figure out what you are going to say.

M: That is it Cindy, you know. That's so amazing that you say that 'cause Cindy when you tell me what I was going to say, it's almost always wrong. I mean it's wrong and it's infuriating and it drives me nuts(.) Like you really know me so well, that you know exactly what I'm going to say. And it's never ever true. It's never the correct answer. It's what you want to believe I'm going to decide.

So I don't know why, so you can feel sorry for yourself or something, but it, you know, it's annoying.

M: And you do it, don't you? A lot.

F: (angrily) Yes, I do it. But I always have a basis for doing it.

M: Why? WHY? Why do you continue to do it? And I always tell you

F: When was the last time you

M: Cindy, and we talked about this so much, and I always tell you,
you know, please, I don't mind doing it, but you continue to, you
continue to second guess me.

F: Last time we got in an argument, one of the things you were mad
about is that I had use of your car and you drove me around like
a chauffeur.

M: When was this? I never said that.

F: Oh, yes, you have.

M: Never.

F: Yes, you have.

M: Never, never, never.
(conflict continues for 15 more turns)

M: Well, obviously, we are not going to agree on this. Don't get angry.
Let's move on. (pp. 404-405)

In this episode, Charles lodges a complaint against Cindy. His
complaint centers on Cindy's tendency to "read his mind," which
of course constitutes an imposition on his negative face. At the
same time, his complaining about Cindy's behavior poses a threat
to her negative face because it expresses a desire to constrain her
behavior. As the episode unfolds, it is apparent that the criticism
implicates Cindy's positive face as well. The complaint about
Cindy's mind reading can be interpreted by Cindy as an indictment of her competence as a communicator. As Cindy gets more
defensive, she performs a behavior that commonly escalates and
diffuses conflict; that is, she shifts the focus to a different issue.

The sort of complaints we are discussing here are distinguish-
able from *general complaining* by someone in a bad mood who is
complaining *to* a partner, but not *about* the partner. Chuck, for
example, may come home from work and proceed to give Dawn,
his wife, an extended rendering of what a lousy day he has had.
"My hemorrhoids were really a pain in the ass today. . . . and then

my boss completely snubbed me when I asked for some help. . . .
and that jerk Jim never returned my call. . . . and those incompetent dweebs at the dry cleaners got a spot on my suit. . . . and . . . "
This might be called "generic bitching and moaning." This generic
complaining is face-threatening to the extent that it imposes on
the partner's patience and expects a sympathetic ear (a topic we
will address shortly), but it is neutral with respect to the partner's
positive face. Complaints to a partner about his or her behavior
(or disposition) are clearly more serious threats to a partner's face.
Susan Shimanoff (1985, 1987) explains that various types of emotional disclosures to a partner (e.g., "You hurt my feelings" or "I'm
mad at you") imply disapproval and thereby threaten the partner's
positive face. Moreover, complaining about the partner potentially poses a challenge to his or her status in the relationship and
thereby calls into question the relationship-specific face. It is not
surprising, then, that complaints can lead to defensive behavior.

All kinds of complaints are not created equal. Some types of
complaints threaten face to a greater degree than others. Alberts
(1989) interviewed couples in an effort to characterize the content
of different kinds of complaints. She identifies five primary complaint types:

1. behavioral (e.g., "Why haven't I had a cooked meal all week?")
2. personal characteristic (e.g., "You're a snob.")
3. performance (e.g., "You're driving too fast.")
4. complaining (e.g., "You're always complaining.")
5. personal appearance (e.g., "You have a fat butt and better lose
   weight.")

In an analysis of couples' interactions during complaint episodes,
Alberts (1988) found that maladjusted (e.g., dissatisfied) couples
were more likely to engage in personal characteristic complaints
than were adjusted couples. Certainly such complaints are among
the most face-threatening, and are most likely to result in defensive responses. Similarly, complaining about a personal characteristic will often be more face-threatening than complaining about
a particular behavior. If a partner is accused of being untrustworthy

or slovenly or dumb, it cuts to the core of his or her identity, and the partner's face is slashed. Such images are unwanted and hurt deeply. If, however, the partner is accused of leaving the cap off the shampoo bottle or not depositing dirty clothes in the hamper, the indictment is peripheral rather than central to the partner's identity. As a practical matter, it is simply more difficult to deny specific identifiable behaviors compared with general personality attributes.

Just as complaints differ in terms of how severely face is threatened, responses to complaints vary with respect to the relative mitigation or aggravation of face threat. Alberts (1989) classifies responses to complaints into five categories:

1. offering an account (e.g., "It's not my fault.")
2. denying the legitimacy of the complaint (e.g., "I do not!")
3. expressing agreement (e.g., "I'm sorry, you're right.")
4. countercomplaining (e.g., "I may leave the cap off the shampoo bottle, but *you* always rudely interrupt me.")
5. passing (i.e., ignoring the complaint or failing to respond verbally)

Behavioral complaints, by far the most frequent type (72% of those reported), are most often responded to with an account. "By both acknowledging the legitimacy of the complaint but also denying culpability for it, the recipient manages to save face for both members of the interaction" (Alberts, 1989, p. 139). Personal characteristic complaints, however, are countered most frequently with denial. As the face-threatening nature of a complaint gets more severe, it is more likely to draw a defensive response designed to protect and save face for the complaint recipient.

Certain patterns of complaints and responses reflect communication that is relatively constructive or relatively destructive for relationships. Alberts and Driscoll (1992) examined the trajectory of couples' complaint episodes to obtain a more macroscopic view of the patterns of conflict involved in managing complaints. Their analysis revealed six different types of complaint episodes exhibited by the married and cohabiting couples in their sample. The episode between Cindy and Charles depicted earlier represents the type labeled *escalated*, which is characterized by expansion of the topic and the hostility level of the complaint interaction. Other conversational complaint episodes identified by Alberts and Driscoll include *passed*, in which the complaint is ignored; *refocused*, in which the focus of the complaint is altered; *mitigated*, in which the severity of the complaint is downgraded; *responsive*, in which the partner's complaint is validated; and *unresponsive*, in which the validity of the partner's complaint is denied. Compared with satisfied couples, these researchers found, dissatisfied couples were more likely to exhibit unresponsive or escalated complaint episodes. Other studies have also found that countercomplaining responses are more common in dissatisfied couples, whereas admitting the legitimacy of a complaint is more common in satisfied couples (Alberts, 1988; Gottman, 1979).

The nature of complaints and the verbal manner in which they are presented affect the relative mitigation or aggravation of face threat in a complaint episode. This is reflected in the complaint behaviors that individuals report they prefer to receive (and not to receive) from their partners. Alberts (1989) asked survey respondents to describe the type of complaint behaviors and complaint response behaviors most desired and least desired from their partners. The most frequently cited behaviors are shown in Tables 4.1 and 4.2. The preferred behaviors are generally those that would be seen as minimizing face threat and keeping discussion focused on the issue raised by the complaint. The least-preferred behaviors, on the other hand, are clearly those that exacerbate the face threat inherent in a complaint and expand conflict to other issues.

Just as important as the content of complaints and responses in determining degree of face threat is their affective tone. Comments that are marked by hostility, animosity, or sarcasm tend to divert the focus of conflict from content issues to face issues. These negative behaviors are disconfirming and provocative. They convey a sense of disrespect and even contempt for the recipient. Nonverbal communication tends to "say" more about a relationship than does verbal communication (see, e.g., Watzlawick, Beavin, & Jackson, 1967). It is therefore not surprising that dissatisfied

Table 4.1 Most- and Least-Preferred Complaint Behaviors Received
              From Partner

Most-Preferred Behaviors	*Least-Preferred Behaviors*
Talking calmly/rationally	Yelling
Being specific/clear/direct	Making personal attacks
Offering complaints constructively	Making indirect complaints
Offering behavioral complaints	Withholding complaints
Saying criticisms nicely	Criticizing/ridiculing
Not complaining at all	Poorly timed complaints

Table 4.2 Most- and Least-Preferred Complaint Responses Received
              From Partner

Most-Preferred Behaviors	*Least-Preferred Behaviors*
Acknowledgment/agreement	Ignoring/passing
Stating calmly	Yelling
Working toward a solution	Arguing
Positive response	Denial
Understanding	Countercomplaining
Focusing on the issue	Becoming defensive
	Justification
	Rudeness
	Hitting

SOURCE: Tables 4.1 and 4.2 are adapted from Alberts's original set of four tables (pp. 136-138) in J. K. Alberts, "A Descriptive Taxonomy of Couples' Complaint Interactions," *Southern Communication Journal*, 1989, Vol. 54, pp. 125-143. Reprinted by permission of The Southern States Communication Association.

couples display negative affect during complaint episodes to a much greater degree than do satisfied couples (Alberts, 1988; Gottman, 1979, 1982).

Clearly, there is some connection between the pattern of complaining in a relationship and the affective climate of that relationship. Episodes of conflict escalate and substantive problem solving derails when the *objective* for one or both partners is to save and defend their *own* faces. The focus of interaction becomes defending the threatened self-concept rather than addressing the source of the complaint. Sometimes, however, this sort of conflict is necessary because the relationship culture is ill-defined or relationship partners need to renegotiate their expectations and mutual definition for the relationship.

Paradoxically, we should note that *not* voicing complaints can be problematic, too. Some relational partners exhibit a reluctance to voice complaints because they fear the consequences of conflict engagement. Michael Roloff and Denise Cloven (1990) refer to this chronic withholding of complaints as a "chilling" effect. They identify three characteristics of chilling. First, the reticent individual is negatively affected by some behavior or trait of the partner. This manifests itself in feelings of anger, frustration, irritation, and so on. Second, the perceived incompatibility is ongoing, but withheld from the offending partner (though it may be revealed to a third party, such as a friend or a counselor). Third, "the basis for not confronting the partner is the fear that conflict escalation might damage the relationship. Whether this fear is an accurate assessment matters little; the individual believes it to be true and withholds the information" (Roloff & Cloven, 1990, p. 51). Over time, the consequences for the overall relationship may be chilling as well. "By not communicating about the problem, the person may be forced to adapt to an ongoing, unpleasant circumstance with growing resentment" (p. 51). If serious areas of disagreement remain unexpressed, then the partners have not negotiated a truly mutual relationship culture. The relationship-specific face is a facade without adequate foundation. The relationship appears much more stable than it actually is.

The role of complaints in interpersonal relationships illustrates the dialectical nature of negotiating a joint identity in the course of developing a close relationship. Some complaints are inevitable and *should* be expressed. Others are probably not worth expressing. What is important is that partners remain sensitive to each other's face, particularly during episodes in which a dissatisfaction relevant to the relationship is being voiced. It is in episodes such as these that the tendency to abandon the cooperative principle of supporting each other's face is heightened.

If complaints are not as bad as the label implies, then social support might be a bit more problematic than we tend to assume at first blush. We turn now to a discussion of this common communication function found in close relationships.

✻ Social Support

One of the interesting ironies of close relationships is that they are capable of being the source of both our greatest pleasure and our greatest pain. As partners come to know each other, they learn about vulnerabilities and "soft spots"; they also begin to "mind read" and make assumptions about what their partners need, even before requests are made or without explicit discussion. This increased real and assumed knowledge makes a close partner a perfect source of social support—sort of. In this section we detail some of the costs that can accrue to both partners during supportive attempts.

By *social support*, we mean the responses that people give to other persons who seem to be distressed, unhappy, suffering from recent traumatic events (e.g., a death in the family), or just generally trying to deal with some problem at home or work (Rook, 1985). Most of these responses are communicative, such as listening sympathetically or offering advice, but some can involve tangible assistance as well. Offering just the right kind of support, in the right way, at the right time is not easy to do. Even before we discuss the scholarly work done on social support, the reader is probably aware of how markedly social support episodes can differ from one another. Some can make a person feel good, because he or she provided or received exactly the right kind of support needed at the time. Some episodes, however, can result in feelings of inadequacy, if a person is unable to give the right kind of support or receives support that makes him or her feel even worse and more incompetent than before the episode. An individual may not even have solicited the supposed support, and may find him- or herself thinking, "What right do you have to say this to me? You could not possibly know how I feel." Sometimes, too, it is not a single episode that goes awry, but the fact that one has listened to a friend or intimate other complain about the same problem over and over. Sometimes one can barely restrain oneself from saying, "Well, then, *do* something about it if you don't like it!"

Readers who recognize these situations in their own lives are aware of the rewards and costs of social support provision. From a face perspective, we might say that the recipient is the principal benefactor, in that positive face needs are met and bolstered, and the provider incurs the greater cost because his or her negative face is greatly constrained by the emotional time and energy that is invested in creating support messages. However, even within this general model there is variation in that some forms of support may actually diminish the recipient's positive and negative face; in addition, when support attempts are merely symbolic or empty gestures, the provider's negative face may not even be implicated.

Social support has enjoyed a great deal of scholarly research, though only occasionally from a face perspective. The more common approaches include (a) measuring the extent to which people perceive themselves to be connected to a social network that could provide specific assistance if requested (e.g., Sarason, Levine, Basham, & Sarason, 1983; Procidano & Heller, 1983) and (b) examining the use and effect of certain types of support messages in particular contexts. In this latter vein, Cutrona, Suhr, and MacFarlane (1990) have summarized a number of support studies and have identified five types of social support messages that underlie support typologies. These include informational support (advice, information about options, and the like), esteem support (validation, assurances of competence and worth), network support (reminders about other people who have had similar experiences or possess relevant expertise), tangible assistance (offers of help, loans, and so on), and emotional support (listening, offering empathy/sympathy, being a confidant).

Some of the items on Cutrona et al.'s list of support messages are clearly inherently face related. As we have discussed in previous chapters, such communicative actions as giving advice threaten negative face of the recipient, just as serving as someone's confidant imposes on negative face of the provider. But validating someone's self-esteem also bolsters positive face.

Scholars have recently begun to integrate the large number of research findings under theoretical frameworks that are very compatible with a face perspective. For example, James Coyne and his colleagues have argued in several publications that social support is a particular type of "dilemma" that has costs and rewards precisely because people are struggling with the multiple needs and goals inherent in relationships (see, e.g., Coyne & De Longis, 1986). According to Coyne, Ellard, and Smith (1990), "social support is best viewed as a general rubric for some of the effects of involvement in social relationships rather than as a working theoretical concept" (p. 129). Similarly, in a book edited by Steve Duck in 1990, a chapter by John La Gaipa and a chapter by Daena Goldsmith and Malcolm Parks both discuss the support episode as an interactional and relational dilemma that reflects the pull between multiple goals and needs, specifically between the poles of two relational dialectics: autonomy-dependency and privacy-intimacy. La Gaipa argues that the negative consequences of not receiving support have been well documented, but the negative effects of receiving support have not been attended to as carefully. He states, "The short-term effects include feeling smothered and controlled, feeling obliged to conform, and a sense of inadequacy, whereas the long-term effects include low self-esteem and identity problems, resentment, and depression" (p. 122).

Goldsmith (1992) proposes the use of face theory as an integrative theoretical framework for social support research. She suggests that researchers separate social support processes into two foci. First, she says, researchers should continue to try to identify the types of messages that most people, *generally, in most contexts*, consider to be supportive messages. These taxonomies (e.g., the Inventory of Socially Supportive Behaviors; Barrera & Ainlay, 1983) are important for constructing instruments to measure the various features that constitute supportive messages.

However, Goldsmith also argues that a second concern is the question of "whether or not the acts succeed in accomplishing the larger outcome of being helpful." In other words, even the best-laid plans of mice and friends sometimes fail. She suggests three conditions that must be met for a message to function supportively. First, the type of assistance offered must be appropriate for the situation. Teasing may help a friend get over the loss of a racquetball game, but not the loss of a lover. Advice may be great for a person who doesn't know what to do, but may be irritating for someone who simply wants to ventilate his or her feelings.

Second, the person giving the support (and, we would add, the person receiving the support) must communicate it in a competent manner. There is probably nothing more disconfirming than a perfunctory proverbial pat on the head when we are truly in need of assistance. If the time is not right for the giving or receiving of support, then perhaps a delay until a more auspicious time will increase the likelihood of providing and accepting support competently. Third, the support effort must meet the goal of satisfying the receiver's face wants as well as the provider's face wants.

According to Goldsmith, this third component, positive and negative face concerns, has been largely ignored in the scholarly literature but is very important for understanding successful support attempts. She traces the importance of face concerns to such features as the ubiquity of face—face needs and face threats are fundamental to supportive interactions because they are fundamental to all interactions. In addition, she points out that face is implied within the very concept of support, because the psychological and physical well-being engendered by supportive communication is made possible because a person is made to feel *accepted* (positive face) and *in control* of his or her emotions and/or circumstances (negative face).

Of particular interest when discussing social support in close relationships is that a traditional view of how the process works— that is, one that is based on social and public interactions—may not capture the nuances of face concerns in close relationships. As each relationship develops its own culture, it adapts and distorts conventional support processes. For example, we would assume that in most ordinary situations, when a person offers tangible assistance with a task or chore, or offers to give or lend money, that the recipient would appreciate the gesture and feel supported. However, in some relationships this type of support serves only to enable the receiver's continued dependency. Likewise, the conventional mechanism of using politeness before threatening a person's positive or negative face may be omitted or reinterpreted in a close relationship. Instead of a partner using several politeness features in a message to soften the imposition of advice, he or she might simply be very direct. So instead of saying, "I don't know if you have thought about this idea, and maybe you have because you tend to think pretty carefully about these matters, but what you might try is XYZ," the partner says, "Well, obviously, what you have to do is XYZ."

Sometimes the norms in a relational culture will make the giving and receiving of support even more difficult, because the norms say something like, *Do not interfere* or *Don't be condescending.* These norms are far below the surface of the relationship, but still constrain how a couple or a family or a group of friends interact.

Interestingly, people develop mechanisms that enable them to deal with norms that are at odds with the ordinary processes of giving and receiving support. An illustration of one such method was discovered in a series of studies of elementary teachers by Glidewell, Tucker, Todt, and Cox (1983). Although these teachers may not be as "intimate" as close friends or romantic partners, they did work together on a daily basis and created a working culture that can be compared with the culture of a close relationship. Glidewell et al. observed that two norms were strongly endorsed by the teachers: that teachers should have equal status and autonomy, and that requesting or offering advice implies superior status for the advice giver. As one may imagine, a teacher in this group who was having some difficulty in the classroom would have been frustrated by trying to follow both of these norms at the same time. What the teachers did to accommodate these competing norms was to rely on "experience swapping," or the sharing of stories and experiences that allowed the troubled teacher to draw out good possible solutions for her problems without having to feel that another teacher acted as a superior by giving explicit advice.

Couples and families develop similar ways to accommodate competing norms, but identifying them is a challenge for researchers because most people are unaware of the regularity of support in their daily interactions. They tend to become aware of it only when a significant event calls for explicit and sophisticated support messages. But most support episodes are actually very brief and idiosyncratic; they might not even be recognized by the partners themselves or by researchers who interview a couple. For example, when a spouse comes home from work and begins to complain about a coworker not pulling his or her share of the load, a partner can lend support merely by listening and validating the legitimacy of the spouse's feelings and the reasonableness of his or her interpretation of the coworker's behavior. This form of support is at the heart of what Burleson (1990) calls "comforting behavior," because it helps put into perspective the disappointment, stresses, and emotional anxieties that we experience from everyday events. Because these interactions tend to be part of ordinary dinner-table conversation, neither person pays much attention to them. Couples who provide comforting messages on a regular basis do not even realize that the implicit validation of each other as competent individuals is actually the ongoing provision of social support.

Of course, sometimes, for whatever reason, the partner who hears the comment about the coworker says something like, "Oh, you always overdramatize everything; I bet Gerry didn't mean a thing by his comment and he was trying to make a contribution to the project by offering to type it." In the cultures of some couples this is humorous, and the complainer acknowledges the likelihood that he or she is overreacting. However, in other relational cultures this response is not supportive at any level. After a long period of such responses, a person may experience lowered relational satisfaction and not quite understand why. The spouse whose feelings and sense of esteem are never validated might even seek other relationships that are more supportive. If another relationship becomes important enough to threaten the primary relationship, the partners may find themselves dealing with a common form of relational transgression.

✍ Relational Transgressions

Relational transgressions are probably easier to recognize after they happen rather than beforehand, because they vary quite a bit among couples who experience them. Although many couples would say that being sexually involved with a person outside of the primary relationship is a transgression, other couples would not. Some couples would also say that being attracted to another person and wanting to date him or her is a transgression, whereas other couples would say that "wanting" to do something is not a transgression unless desires become actions. Within this latter group, however, there may be an understanding that such desires must be talked about and, if not, the omission becomes the transgression. In addition, for these couples, if the third party of interest happens to be a former lover, then the sense of transgression might increase.

Why are there differences in what couples consider to be relational transgressions? Part of the answer lies in the fact that actions, attitudes, and values become transgressions only when one or both partners consider them to be *violations of some rule of conduct or taken-for-granted expectation about how the partners should act in their relationship.*

When a couple builds a relational culture together, they create both explicit norms for behavior and implicit expectations that might not even be recognized until a violation occurs. The norms and expectations in their culture derive in part from the broader domain of social and relational face discussed earlier, but are uniquely constituted at the level of relationship-specific face. When one partner transgresses, the stability of this culture is threatened. The severity of the threat to the relationship will depend upon the degree to which the infraction calls into question the integrity or validity of the couple's jointly created relationship-specific face.

In this section we will examine three ways in which face and facework help us understand the occurrence of transgressions and the process of coping with them once they are revealed or discovered. First, we examine how certain kinds of actions threaten relationship-specific face and thereby function as transgressions. We also look at specific types of actions to see how these implicate the positive and negative face of the individuals in the relationship, thereby functioning as transgressions at an individual level. Second, we explore the emotions that often arise from knowledge of transgressions, particularly such emotions as jealousy (for the offended partner) and shame or guilt (for the transgressor), to determine how these emotions are related to face loss. Finally, we analyze the predicament that arises when a transgression is revealed or discovered in order to see how facework is used to salvage the transgressor's integrity and/or the viability of the relationship.

Relationship Transgressions as Face Threats

A relational transgression threatens face at two levels: the relationship and the individual. The more abstract level is the jointly constructed relationship-specific face. Goffman (1959) uses the word "team" to refer to a pair or group who present a unified image or identity to the public. He says that if even one member does not play his or her part properly, the performance of the whole team is impaired. Anyone who has ever played on a team can appreciate Goffman's analogy.

Let us extend this analogy to a relationship. If Kim and Dan have a close relationship, part of their public and private performance (in Goffman's sense) depends upon the shared understanding of how each will behave and what each will value. If Kim learns from her friends that Dan was seen at dinner with another woman, she might initially think little of it. If it happened several times, she might begin to feel her relationship-specific face is being threatened because Dan is violating a "free-time rule" as Kim sees it. She assumes that when two people are a couple, they want to spend any free time they might have with each other. At this level, Dan might be able to apologize to Kim and either abide more carefully by the free-time rule or ask if it could be renegotiated. This is a relatively minor threat to the joint identity of the relationship because it is only a rule of time allocation that does not call into question whether Kim and Dan are still a couple.

On the other hand, if Kim also learns that Dan has been involved sexually with this other woman, Kim may find that an apology and renegotiation of the exclusivity rule is not appropriate, and she will exit the relationship. For Kim, the assumptions that constituted the relationship's "identity" no longer hold. In terms of the team metaphor, Dan is trying to execute the same play with two pass receivers, and Kim recognizes that this will discredit her performance. In addition, the knowledge of Dan's behavior among the social network will discredit Kim's exclusive claim to the role of Dan's partner. In a sense, a serious rival puts a current partner in the awkward position of being "out of face" if he or she claims to be the only partner. Often, the embarrassment that stems from finding out about a sexual transgression of one's partner comes from having been performing a role to which one did not have exclusive right. Ellis and Weinstein (1986) note in a similar vein that people often report jealousy arising in response to threats to one's public identity as a member of a couple—even when there is little strong affection for the partner.

In addition to threatening the face of the relationship, in the sense of invalidating its identity, certain types of behavior also threaten the positive and negative faces of the individuals involved. For example, if Dan indiscriminately shares a confidence from Kim with his friends or breaks a promise he made to her, Kim's positive face wants are violated. These violations are not merely instances of violating a rule of conduct, they are also indications of disregard for Kim's personhood.

Readers can probably think of other examples of threats to individual face. Table 4.3 gives a number of examples of relational transgressions that were provided by 211 college students who were asked to list behaviors, actions, or attitudes that they would consider transgressions if performed (or endorsed) by a romantic partner (Metts, 1991). As one might expect, sexual infidelity was the most often mentioned example of a transgression. However, other sorts of "untoward relational acts" were also mentioned.

"Not trusting and being jealous" can be seen as a threat to the negative face of the recipient because he or she may feel great imposition in trying to avoid any behavior that might give the imposing partner reason to be upset. "Not being there in time of one's partner's need" and "nonreciprocal expressivity" (i.e., not reciprocating terms of affection, such as "I love you") may also be viewed as threats to positive face. Two scholars who have worked for some time in the related areas of sexual affairs and jealousy,

Table 4.3 Behaviors Listed by Respondents as Relational
Transgressions (in percentages)

Sexual intercourse	18
Wanting to or dating others	15
Deception	13
Flirting/necking/petting	10
Violating a confidence	6

Mentioned by at least 5% of respondents
    Forgetting plans and special occasions
    Violating privacy of relationship to network
    Emotional attachment to former partner
    Sex with former partner
    Nonreciprocal expressivity
    Not trusting/being jealous
    Breaking a significant promise
    Changing important plans
    Being physically abusive
    Not being there for the partner during a time of need
    Not fighting fair (intentionally bringing up partner's past mistakes during
       arguments)
    Making unfair comparisons (comparing current relationship and partner to
       former)

SOURCE: Metts (1991).

Bram Buunk and Robert Bringle (1987), suggest that extradyadic affairs threaten positive face when (a) the offended person might be considered responsible for the situation by the network and even the offended person (e.g., he or she did not invest time or attention in the relationship), (b) the event calls into question the image of the offended person as an adequate partner, and (c) the threat from the rival is high.

This leads us to consider the important role of emotions that arise from transgressions. Both the transgressor and the offended partner feel strong emotions that must be recognized and managed, or even more face will be lost. As Goffman (1967) observes in his essay on facework, part of what we mean by the term *dignity* is the ability to control our emotions in face-threatening situations.

Emotions

Jealousy is probably the predominant emotion associated with transgressions, given that many transgressions take the form of third-party involvement. Responses to jealousy have been distinguished as those focused on retaining the relationship and those focused on protecting one's image or esteem (Brehm, 1985; Buunk & Bringle, 1987). Some responses protect both foci, such as when a couple talks candidly about the event and the jealous response, but does so in a face-preserving way. Some responses preserve neither the relationship nor the jealous partner's image, such as when he or she makes a public display of emotion so inappropriate that everyone is embarrassed and the transgressing partner exits the relationship anyway. Some responses preserve the relationship but do so at the cost of the jealous partner's esteem, for example, clinging to and begging the partner not to exit. Finally, some responses allow a jealous person to preserve his or her image, but cost the relationship. Examples of this would include dating someone else to evoke counterjealousy and discrediting the reputation of the transgressing partner by making private information public. These are very similar to the type of facework that Goffman (1967) calls "aggressive" facework, because they attempt to "get back at" the transgressing partner through blame and discrediting. Responding to strong feelings of jealousy poses a serious predicament for the person who would like to preserve both the relationship and his or her image.

Interestingly, the person evoking the jealousy also faces a predicament. It is possible for the social network to make negative attributions about a person whose transgressions have been verified. If the relationship is not important, he or she may exit the relationship and thereby negate any "right" the jealous person might have to feel victimized (e.g., "You have no right to be angry; I'm not your girlfriend anymore"). The transgressor might also point out the role of the jealous partner in "causing" the transgression (e.g., "She deserved it"; "She always wanted her freedom but wouldn't let me do anything").

However, if the relationship means anything at all to the transgressor, he or she is likely to feel guilt and/or shame. These emotions may seem very similar to most readers because they are both negative affective states, but they are different in important ways. In the case of guilt, the transgressor feels tension, remorse, and discomfort because he or she has performed an act that violates an internal standard. It was a "bad thing" to do (or not do), and it seems the only way to reduce the negative feeling is to repair the damage that was done. In the case of shame, the experience is even worse because the entire self is implicated rather than just a single deed. A person who feels shame has lost his or her integrity within a "community" of important others. Tangney (1992) describes the feeling as a "sense of shrinking, of being small, of being worthless and powerless." She says, "whereas guilt motivates a desire to repair, shame motivates a desire to hide—to sink into the floor and disappear" (p. 199). A person who has committed a transgression, whether one of infidelity or some other infraction, may feel guilt and be able to "repair" the transgression through discussions with his or her partner. Shame will not likely follow unless the transgression is serious and made known to members of the network who consider it a moral issue that calls the transgressor's integrity into question.

We recognize that many other emotions in addition to jealousy, guilt, and shame might be stimulated by a transgression. Anger, hurt, resentment, fear, and other emotions are certainly common in most people's experience, and expressing these emotions appropriately is very much a matter of managing face and maintaining dignity. We have focused on jealousy, guilt, and shame, however, because they are so directly tied to the loss of face.

Managing the Revelation/Discovery of a Transgression

Although each interaction during which a couple deals with a transgression will be unique in some regard, we can make a general claim about how the revelation episode will likely unfold. We can say the severity of the transgression will predict the intensity of the emotional reaction, but the investment of the couple in the relationship will predict their willingness to engage in a remedial interchange and mutually supportive facework (Metts & Mongeau, 1991). In other words, when a transgression is very severe, such as sexual infidelity or a major deception, the offended partner will be very emotional (as will the transgressor), but in highly invested relationships, the couple will not simply dissolve the relationship but will try to work out the issues involved.

In this section we present a summary of the types of strategies couples report using when one partner has been found to have committed a transgression. The particular type of transgression we use for purposes of illustration is deception.

Metts, Aune, and Ebesu (1990) asked 145 community adults who were living in Honolulu, Hawaii, to describe the episodes that unfolded when they or their partners were found to have been deceptive. Although the response categories generated were generally consistent with the predicament literature, some emerged that had not previously been represented. Moreover, some responses were found more likely to be used *after* the initial encounter than during. These response categories are listed in Table 4.4.

The most common responses in the initial episode of the discovery of deception reflected several goals of a person in a predicament: (a) the need to control attributions about one's identity (reflected in the strategies of impression management, telling the truth, and providing an excuse), (b) the need to control the extent of one's involvement in the remedial interchange and forestall possible contributions of culpability (reflected in the strategy of refusal/deny), and (c) the need to control one's nonverbal displays (reflected in the strategy of affective state/arousal). These strategies together accounted for 72% of all strategies used in the immediate context.

By contrast, the cluster of strategies most often reported after the revelation event tends to represent concern for restoring, revitalizing, or reaffirming the relationship. Relationship-focused strategies include both fairly passive approaches to restoring the status quo (reflected in the strategy of avoidance/evasion) and more active or explicit approaches (reflected in the strategy of

Table 4.4 Responses to Deceptive Episodes

During initial encounter	
Truth	telling the truth; continued honesty within the relationship ("I decided to be totally honest.")
Apology	expressions of regret or self-castigation that accompany direct or indirect acceptance of responsibility for the deception ("I'm sorry, please forgive me."), sometimes with a promise of better behavior in the future ("I assured him that it would never happen again.")
Excuse	statements that minimize the deceiver's responsibility for the deceptive act, both through appeal to inability ("I didn't know how to tell you.") and through shifting the blame to other people, including the target ("I couldn't tell you because I knew you would get mad and make a scene.")
Justification	statements that accept responsibility for the deceptive act but minimize the pejorative nature of the original event or of the decision to be deceptive ("I told him it was no big deal"; "I said that I was going to tell her later anyway so it wasn't really deception.")
Refusal/denial	verbal or nonverbal attempts to manage the extent of explicit revelation during discussions of the deceptive act; include such practices as failing to provide an account when challenged by the target (e.g., sitting in silence), denying that a deception has occurred ("That's not what I said."), and intentionally omitting undiscovered aspects of the truth ("I did admit to seeing Doug, but I didn't reveal everything that happened.")
Impression management	statements or behaviors designed to repair or reestablish a threatened image or to create a situation-specific image ("I acted guilty"; "I acted innocent"; "I acted angry as though unjustly accused."); statements or behaviors designed to arouse empathy, understanding, or forgiveness for deceiver ("I tried to get her to forgive me"; "I tried to get him to understand my position.")
Relationship invocation	statements or behaviors expressing attitudes or beliefs about the relationship, or invoking qualities of the relationship in order to use it as a frame for

(continued)

Table 4.4 Continued

	interpreting the deceptive act ("We are strong enough to talk this out"; "If our relationship were important, this wouldn't be an issue.")
Affective state/arousal	references to an emotional state or leakage cue (e.g., crying) or references to a loss of control over verbal and/or nonverbal behavior (e.g., stuttering, stammering)
After initial encounter	
Avoidance/evasion	efforts to avoid references to or discussions of the deception and/or the confrontation episode; implicit is the belief that the consequences of the deceptive act can be minimized by allowing it to fade into relational history and conducting the business of the relationship as though nothing had happened ("I tried to avoid bringing it up"; "We just went on as though it had never happened.")
Soothing	statements or behaviors intended to placate or ingratiate the target ("I complimented her more often"; "I tried to be more attentive to his needs."); statements or behaviors that express empathy, sympathy, or validation for the other ("You have every right to be angry.")
Relational work	explicit efforts to reaffirm or strengthen the intensity or stability of the relational bonds ("We spent more time together"; "I called her more often"; "I told him I loved him a lot.")
Relational rituals	normative or ritualistic behavior directed toward appeasing the target or acknowledging the relationship (e.g., gifts, flowers, candy)
Metatalk	explicit discussion of the deception and its impact on the relationship ("We talked about it.")

SOURCE: Metts et al. (1990).

relationship work). There was also an increase in attention and solicitous behavior toward partner (reflected in the strategy of soothing). These strategies together accounted for 71% of all strategies used over time to repair the relationship.

We interpret these findings as evidence that when a relationship is traumatized by the occurrence of a serious transgression, the transgressor will attempt to restore both his or her loss of face and the loss of face for partner. Moreover, once the initial remedial episode has been enacted, the transgressor will also attempt to restore integrity of the relationship.

It appears also that these strategies do work in the manner they are intended. Metts et al. (1990) found that regardless of the type of transgression being described, respondents who reported the use of apology and impression management were more likely to restore trust to their relationship compared with respondents who did not use apology and impression management. This finding is particularly informative about the function of identity management strategies in regaining an identity-relevant attribute such as trust. Apologies not only express sorrow and regret, they also separate the wayward self from the redeemed self (Goffman, 1967) and project a self who promises more acceptable behavior in the future. Similarly, the "posturing" that is characteristic of impression management represents a concerted effort to create an identity consistent with the content of the messages being sent. Goffman (1967) refers to the content as "cues given" to underscore that it is information given intentionally; he refers to the unintentional information about ourselves that we "leak" during interaction as "cues given off." Consistency between cues given (e.g., stating "I love you") and cues given off (e.g., longing eye gaze) is fundamental to reestablishing trust.

Buunk and Bringle (1987) point out that face management strategies must be considered in light of the other partner. That is, if an offended partner will not accept the excuse or justification offered by the transgressor, then it has little or no effect. In essence, Buunk and Bringle say, a couple who are cooperating in managing a transgression revelation episode will jointly construct an "account" and will be more or less supportive of each other's efforts to modify the account until it is mutually acceptable. The "more or less" supportive nature of their interaction will arise from such features as the severity of the transgression. For example, when a transgression is minor, the offended partner will help create a reasonable account (e.g., "I know you didn't expect things to turn out this way; let's see what we can do to fix them"). When a transgression is very severe, the offended partner is less likely to assist in constructing the account (e.g., "You'd better have a good explanation for this one!").

❧ Summary

Earlier, we indicated that face concerns are present in all relationships. As a relationship develops and intimacy grows, some forms of face threat evaporate because the rules of the negotiated relationship culture supersede the original rules of honoring social face. The negotiated relational culture, however, entails some new complexities in facework commensurate with the emergence of relationship-specific face. Moreover, the subtle and tacit defining of a relationship is dynamic and ever evolving. Face is open to renegotiation in virtually any communicative encounter between relational partners. In this chapter, we have explored three types of episodes that constantly challenge the complexion of relationship-specific face, and hence the composition of shared relational culture. Complaints, social support, and relational transgressions are among the various natural and inevitable problematic episodes in close relationships. If relationships are to be sustained, partners must be able to grapple routinely with the challenges of face threat represented by these (and other) problematic episodes. When one or both partners are either unwilling or unable to manage these situations constructively, it may signal the demise of the relationship. Disengaging from a relationship involves its own set of face management challenges; we consider these matters in Chapter 5.

5

Facework in Relationship Disengagement

Ending a relationship is perhaps one of the most face-threatening situations we encounter. Although it may seem that only the person who is being left behind suffers face threat, in reality, the person who initiates the disengagement also feels face threat. As you will recall, when a person's sense of worth and self-esteem are diminished, that person experiences positive face threat; when a person's movements and behavioral intentions are constrained, that person experiences negative face threat. Consider the following scenario:

Johnny and Mary have been dating for three months. Johnny has become bored with the relationship and finds Mary less exciting than several other women who interest him. He is beginning to find that spending time with Mary is more of an obligation than a pleasure.

Which of the following options is most face-preserving for Mary?

1. Johnny simply avoids Mary by not calling or answering the telephone until Mary gets the hint.
2. Johnny sends Mary a letter stating his decision that the relationship is terminated.
3. Johnny asks Mary to meet with him in a quiet place and explains how he feels about the relationship.

Even Dear Abby would recognize that option 3 is the most face-preserving for Mary. The first option is "kind" to the extent that Mary does not have to hear the termination directly—she merely has to infer that the relationship is no longer viable. This indirectness gives Mary maximum flexibility to create the "cover story" of the breakup, both to herself and to the social network. Thus her negative face is enhanced and her positive face is threatened only indirectly. The problem is, however, that Mary is never accorded an explanation for the termination. As Leslie Baxter (1985) argues, when a relationship has been intimate, a dissatisfied partner owes it to the other to at least account directly for his or her intention to end the relationship. To leave the partner in an ambiguous state by simply avoiding contact seems to say that there was never a relationship worth mentioning— a fundamental devaluing for the person who liked the relationship and wanted to maintain it. In addition, the ambiguity leaves the partner open to severe face threat from awkward situations, such as encountering the believed-to-be-my-partner individual out on a date with another person.

Option 2 is more direct and eliminates some of the problems described for option 1. However, because it is what Baxter calls a "fait accompli" or unilateral declaration of the intent to disengage, it devalues Mary as an equal partner in the dissolution process. It does not allow her to express her feelings. Thus her positive face is only somewhat less threatened than in option 1, but her negative face is much more threatened because the decision has been imposed on her and she has no choice but to accept it.

Option 3 does make the "rejection" of Mary as a relational partner explicit, but it also indicates regard for the relationship as something worth discussing, and it indicates regard for Mary's right to participate in the termination process. The account is thereby jointly constructed.

Now, as one more test of your understanding of positive and negative face, choose the option that is most face-threatening for Johnny. If you said option 3, you are correct. When he opens the issue of relationship dissolution, he exposes himself to Mary's opinions about his actions—opinions he could avoid if he chose option 1. Moreover, his negative face is severely threatened by the need to invest his time and energy in meeting with Mary, choosing his words carefully, juggling his goals with her feelings, and so forth—investments that he would not have to make if he simply avoided Mary or wrote her a letter. Many people in Johnny's position would not invest the effort in a face-to-face meeting no matter what the circumstances, because they are so uncomfortable in face-threatening encounters. Other people in Johnny's position would consider nothing less than a face-to-face encounter because they believe in total openness in relationships. Most of us are somewhere in the middle; we consider the circumstances when we consider how to disengage a relationship. For example, if a relationship is highly invested, we will consider it worth the effort of a face-to-face discussion. If we consider it casual, we might not.

In this chapter we introduce the principles that seem to guide people's decisions about how to balance their desire to terminate a relationship with their desire to preserve their own and their partners' face. Researchers who are interested in relationship termination have attempted to identify the strategies that couples use to break up. We will examine these strategies to determine which are the most "polite" in terms of preserving face of both partners.

✖ Typologies of Disengagement Strategies

The scholarly literature on disengagement strategies is confusing at present because writers have used similar terms to describe slightly different types of strategies or have used different terms to describe similar strategies. Michael Cody and his colleagues have proposed five general categories for disengagement strategies (see, e.g., Banks, Altendorf, Greene, & Cody, 1987; Cody, 1982):

1. avoidance ("I didn't say anything to the partner. I avoided contact with him/her as much as possible.")
2. negative identity management ("I told him/her that I was going to date other people and that I thought he/she should date others also.")
3. justification ("I fully explained why I felt dissatisfied with the relationship, that it hasn't been growing and that I believe we will both be happier if we don't date anymore.")
4. de-escalation ("I told him/her that I need to be honest and suggested that we break it off for a while and see what happens.")
5. positive tone ("I told him/her that I was very, very sorry about breaking off the relationship.")

Baxter and her colleagues have asked college students and dating couples in long-distance relationships how they terminated their relationships (see, e.g., Baxter, 1982; Wilmot, Carbaugh, & Baxter, 1985). Much like Cody and his colleagues, they created a list of these strategies. However, over time, Baxter (1985, 1987) realized that these individual strategies could be sorted into clusters according to where they fell along three dimensions:

1. direct to indirect
2. unilateral to bilateral
3. other-orientation to self-orientation

These dimensions yield six clusters of strategies, as shown in Table 5.1.

ᴥ A Model of Politeness and Disengagement

Although Baxter's typology implies that people disengaging from a relationship would select strategies that afford them the most flexibility in reaching their goals, she does not identify

Table 5.1 Disengagement Strategies

Indirect/unilateral
  Withdrawal
    lessens intimacy or frequency of contact
  Pseudo-de-escalation
    false declaration of wanting to retain some level of relationship
  Cost escalation
    makes cost of being in relationship high through rude or hostile actions

Indirect/bilateral
  Mutual pseudo-de-escalation
    both partners pretend that some level of commitment will be retained
  Fading away
    implicit understanding that relationship is over

Direct/unilateral
  Fait accompli
    simple statement that the relationship is over; no account, no discussion
  State-of-the-relationship talk
    explicit statement of dissatisfaction and desire to exit within the context of
    a bilateral discussion of the relationship's problems

Direct/bilateral
  Attributional conflict
    agreeing that breakup is necessary but arguing about the reasons; placing
    blame
  Negotiated farewell
    explicit communication about the relationship and termination;
    sense-making session without blame

Self-orientation
  Cost escalation
  Fait accompli
  Withdrawal
  Attributional conflict

Other-orientation
  State-of-the-relationship talk
  Pseudo-de-escalation
  Bilateral pseudo-de-escalation
  Fading away
  Negotiated farewell

specific features that might influence this decision. Fortunately, if we reflect on the premises that underlie politeness theory, we are able to create a model that helps explain why people choose particular strategies to disengage from relationships.

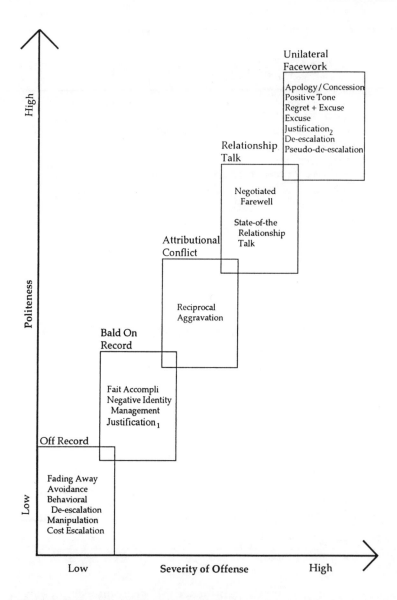

Figure 5.1. Politeness and Disengagement

SOURCE: Metts (1992). Reprinted by permission.
NOTE: Justification$_1$ refers to a disengagement strategy defined by Cody (1982) and Justification$_2$ refers to a type of account defined by Scott and Lyman (1968).

Figure 5.1 depicts a model of the expected relationships among three components according to politeness theory: (a) the seriousness of the "offense" of breaking up, (b) a type of message (e.g., an excuse) or a type of episode (e.g., negotiated farewell), and (c) the degree of politeness in the message or episode. The fundamental assumption is that as the seriousness of the event (i.e., the breakup) increases, the greater the weight placed on hearer support, thereby increasing the likelihood of polite disengagement strategies. The seriousness of the breakup will increase as a function of several factors, including, for example, how long a couple has been dating or married, how much network overlap they share, how enmeshed they have become (children, home, property), and how strongly the dissolution is desired by one partner relative to the other.

Off-Record Strategies

We begin movement through the model in the lower left-hand corner, where severity of offense is low. Severity may be low for at least two reasons. First, it may be low because the relationship never progressed very far; it turned out to be a typical sort of situation where after one or two interactions it was clear that there was no chance for much of a relationship to develop. Although we might argue that a disengager should always be up-front about the intention not to continue the relationship, at least in this case we can understand that the senses of obligation and guilt are low. Second, a relationship might have been very highly developed, and the disengager may have tried over and over to be direct in his or her breakup strategies, but these attempts failed. The frustration leads the disengager to feel that he or she has tried to be up-front and now has every right to be indirect and simply withdraw from all contact. The strategies most likely to occur in this area are indirect, primarily passive, strategies. They have been referred to by various names, including withdrawal, manipulation, drifting apart, cost escalation, and behavioral de-escalation (Banks et al., 1987; Baxter, 1985).

In this quadrant of the model, politeness is also low. This might seem contrary to what we said in Chapter 1 about "going off record" (hinting) being inefficient, but face-preserving. The model associates off-record strategies with low politeness because disengagement is a special kind of face-threatening situation. During disengagement, some degree of directness indicates politeness because the disengager is willing to threaten his or her own negative face needs to acknowledge the positive face needs of the other person. According to Baxter (1987), "The other's positive face is threatened under any circumstance, but the threat is probably greatest with Distance Cueing [off-record strategies], for it doesn't even show the basic courtesy of a face-to-face accounting" (p. 207). In addition, Brown and Levinson (1987) state that directness is sometimes polite if being indirect will lead to face threat at a later time. That is often the case with disengagement. If a person is extremely indirect in his or her intention to break up, it could lead to very embarrassing situations for both people. Ambiguous relationship definition is uncomfortable; one doesn't know what to tell friends when they ask, or how to act when one meets the other person in public.

The association in the model between off-record strategies and low politeness is also supported by empirical research, though the support is indirect. No one has assessed perceived politeness when these strategies are used, but related data suggest that they are not perceived favorably by users or recipients. Metts, Cupach, and Bejlovec (1989) found that withdrawal was negatively associated with postdisengagement friendship for the initiator of a breakup. Wilmot et al. (1985) found that when disengagers used withdrawal, they reported that they did not feel good about the breakup and expressed regrets for using that strategy.

One set of off-record strategies, labeled "cost escalation" by Baxter, seems to be particularly low in politeness. In cost escalation, an individual acts rudely or callously in a relationship to the point where the other person finds the cost to his or her ego and peace of mind too great to stay in the relationship. In a study of postdisengagement friendship, the person who was broken up with was significantly less likely to remain friends with a former romantic partner when that person used cost escalation (e.g., intentionally breaking dates) than with any other strategy (Metts et al., 1989). Although cost escalation strategies allow the disengager to avoid confrontation, they force the other party into the position of having to go on record with the disengagement message. Thus cost escalation implicates not only the positive face of partner in the use of hostile acts and/or demeaning actions, but also the negative face of partner because he or she has to orchestrate the disengagement. Ironically, cost escalation is also threatening to the positive face of the user, because he or she must create the image of a person not worthy of being a relational partner (Baxter, 1987). Observers would quite likely see the person using cost escalation as both "heartless" and "shameless" in Goffman's (1967) sense of the terms.

On-Record Strategies

Going on record with a face-threatening act—that is, actually confronting one's partner when one wants to break up—is more difficult to do than simply withdrawing without contact. A disengager will not exert the effort unless he or she feels there is something to be gained. As one might imagine, what a person gains are clarity (about his or her feelings, so that there is no ambiguity) and attributions of honesty and outspokenness. What he or she avoids from members of the social network are attributions of being a coward and being manipulative (Brown & Levinson, 1987). Baxter (1987) notes that on-record strategies demonstrate to the social network that the disengager has displayed concern for the other's face appropriate to the obligations that accompany close relationships.

There are several types of on-record strategies, and some are not as polite as others. *Bald* (nonredressed) on-record strategies are blunt and unelaborated statements that the relationship is over. Among these strategies are fait accompli, negative identity management, and justification. These strategies are indeed efficient and unambiguous. They do indicate enough respect for the relationship and for partners to confront the dissolution directly. However, bald on-record strategies are placed relatively low in politeness on the model, as they do not redress the recipient's positive face needs through apologies or accounts, nor do they redress the recipient's negative face by allowing his or her participation in the decision to disengage.

We would expect bald on-record strategies to be used when the relationship is developed enough to deserve a formal exit, but not emotionally or structurally enmeshed enough to make the breakup seem overly serious. The disengager may also feel exempt from guilt and obligation because he or she believes the partner is at fault for the breakup. This notion has been supported by the findings in a study by Banks et al. (1987), who found that disengagers used negative identity management strategies to dissolve relationships when they felt the partner was responsible. For instance, recall the section on relational transgressions in Chapter 4: It is easy to imagine that discovering one's partner has been unfaithful would lead one to feel justified in ignoring the face needs of the partner.

Though it may seem to be justified, the lack of politeness associated with bald on-record strategies makes them a somewhat dangerous choice as a disengagement tool. Such strategies are indeed efficient, but the damage to face makes them costly. Wilmot et al. (1985) found that people who used a bald on-record strategy they label "verbal directness" to terminate a relationship reported negative emotional reactions to the termination. These authors argue that excessive bluntness boomerangs and produces negative reactions for the user as well as the recipient.

Going on record with redressive action is represented in the model by three boxes. The first is labeled with Baxter's term "attributional conflict." As defined by Baxter, attributional conflict indicates that both parties have agreed on the need for dissolution but have not agreed on the reasons. Although Baxter does not identify specific strategies that might be used in attributional conflict, it is likely that each partner blames the other. Thus there might be complaint and countercomplaint sequences; there might be accusations and denials. Whatever the particular pattern, more effort is spent on placing blame for the past than on negotiating the future.

We would expect to find attributional conflict episodes in relationships where termination is a relatively severe offense. It is unlikely that a couple would invest the time and effort to identify the cause of dissolution unless loss of the relationship is perceived as significant. Interestingly, the model indicates that politeness is greater for attributional conflict than for bald on-record strategies. This may seem counterintuitive, but it is based on the assumption that bilateral disengagement, even when conflictual, redresses at least the negative face needs of both parties because both participate in the disengagement discussion. In addition, because both parties have agreed that dissolution is desirable, the threat to positive face is less than in unilateral withdrawal.

The second box for on record with redressive action, labeled "relationship talk," is also based on Baxter's work and contains the two types of episodes she has identified. As with attributional conflict, Baxter has not recorded specific strategies occurring within these types of episodes, but we can infer that they are more face redressive than in attributional conflict. Not only is the decision to disengage from the relationship a bilateral one, but the reasons are not in dispute, so there is no blaming. In fact, when both partners agree that the reasons are external to the couple, they tend to be very direct in their discussion of disengagement (Baxter, 1982). Obviously, there is much less face threat in saying good-bye because one person takes a job out of state than there is in saying good-bye because one partner has fallen in love with someone else. Whatever the reason for the breakup, both parties agree that it should end and work together to negotiate a mutually satisfying dissolution of the relationship. Because this effort is usually extended in well-developed relationships, the seriousness is high, and because the relationship is jointly deconstructed in a face-preserving way, the politeness is also high.

The final cluster of strategies is called "unilateral facework" because it contains strategies most explicitly redressive to the face needs of the recipient. In these situations, disengagement is desired by one person in the relationship, and he or she perceives the exit to be a severe offense. The seriousness might stem from the fact that the relationship is well developed, the disengager feels guilt because the breakup is unilateral, or the disengager perhaps fears retribution from the deserted partner.

The strategies included here form two clusters. De-escalation, pseudo-de-escalation, and justification are strategies that request redefinition (rather than termination) of the relationship. These strategies attempt to compensate for loss of positive face implied in the disengager's decision to leave the relationship by expressing continued desire to be in a relationship, to be friends, and to be affiliated. Banks et al. (1987) found that disengagers are more likely to use positive tone, de-escalation, or justification when network overlap is high, the relationship is intimate, and postdisengagement friendship is desired. That is, people use positive tone and de-escalation tactics to reduce the level of intimacy in the relationship while attempting to keep some kind of relationship alive, and they do so when the partner is not blamed for the costs in the relationship and there is a chance to increase intimacy at a later time.

Another cluster of strategies is made up of excuses, excuses plus regrets, positive tone strategies, and apologies. These all express strong regard for the esteem aspect of the recipient's positive face (as opposed to the affiliation aspect noted above). Apologies not only express regret, but ask forgiveness. Excuses attempt to say that the decision is a serious one but cannot be helped; it is out of the disengager's control. And justifications attempt to reframe the dissolution so that it is not so face-threatening. For example, one might say, "This is not a rejection of you; I still care about you. I just need time to learn about myself." What all the strategies included here have in common is a focus on the face needs of the other person at the expense of the face needs of the disengager.

Both clusters of strategies are associated with high politeness. Apologies and concessions, for example, are considered to be highly deferential (e.g., Schlenker & Darby, 1981; Schonbach, 1980). Holtgraves (1989) found the regret plus excuse to be more satisfying to hearers than any other facework strategy, and Metts et al. (1989) found that when an initiator used positive tone strategies, the couple was more likely to remain friends after the breakup.

❧ Summary

As you review the model presented here, consider how well it seems to capture your own intuitive and experiential understanding of relationship disengagement. Have you ever been avoided by someone whom you considered a relational partner only to learn later that he or she considered your relationship terminated? Would you have preferred a more direct accounting? Have you found it generally true that in more developed relationships there seems to be greater obligation to support face, both for the leaver and for the person left behind? Do you generally find that when one person has made a unilateral decision to terminate a relationship, particularly when it is a well-developed one, he or she uses very elaborated messages with apologies and accounts? There is probably some guilt in these cases, and guilt can be a strong motivator to put effort into explaining a decision.

Do you find anything missing from the model? We do. The model fails to give much attention to the responses of the person who is broken up with in the unilateral situation. There are at least two reactions we might have shown for the person who receives the elaborated messages in the top box. This person might reject even the most apologetic and supplicatory strategy and not allow the disengager to make a graceful exit. In a sense, such a response would be aggressive facework to impugn the face of the disengager, either in person or through negative stories in the social network. On the other hand, the person being left behind sometimes displays incredible willingness to support the face of the disengager. It is the stuff of motion-picture sentiment to see a gallant young man say to his beloved as she leaves him for another man that her happiness is all that matters. Most of us are less lofty and find such support difficult to give when we feel diminished.

Second, the model appears to be static when, in fact, disengagement is quite dynamic. People move in and out of the various boxes as the process unfolds. Thus a relationship that was cherished and special may become ordinary and problematic as it unravels. Hence efforts to be face-preserving early in the process may finally give way to direct and bald on-record strategies later.

Similarly, relationship talk might eventually give way to attributional conflict. However, the reverse might also happen. Relationship talk might reveal to a couple how very special the relationship is and, rather than disengage, the couple might repair the relationship.

Third, the concept of seriousness of offense requires specification. Current disengagement research has examined the influence of network overlap, reasons for disengagement, attitudes toward partner's role, and degree of intimacy. In the service of heurism, the model presumes a sort of linear combination of these variables contributing to total seriousness. In reality, each of these variables merits independent and conjoint examination to determine its relative importance in how a person assesses the seriousness of ending a particular relationship.

6

Relationships
About Face

Our goal in this book has been to sketch the outlines of a theory we believe is useful for understanding certain important phenomena in interpersonal relationships. The theory focuses on the concept of face and is based on the premise that "the desire to gain face, to avoid losing face, and to save face when it is threatened is a powerful social motive" (Ho, 1976, p. 883). Although the theory was originally developed to explain social interaction more generally, our aim has been to stretch and adapt the framework to processes exhibited in close relationships.

Whenever people communicate with one another, face is relevant. But face concerns are particularly salient in "problematic" episodes and types of interaction. Hence we believe the concepts of face and facework are especially potent when employed to make sense out of situations where individuals find interaction with a partner to be challenging, threatening, paradoxical, difficult, or awkward. We therefore have applied the theory to problematic episodes involved in the construction, maintenance, and erosion of interpersonal relationships. The theory is not intended to be— nor, in our opinion, should it be taken to be—an all-encompassing grand explanation of social and personal relationships.

The analyses we have presented in these chapters also have been illustrative and suggestive, rather than intensive and definitive. Many of the claims we have made are consistent with existing empirical research, whereas others are speculative; few are the result of direct attempts to validate or falsify face management theory. We hope that the contours of the theory outlined in this book will serve as a springboard for more precise and elaborate articulation of its workings in particular problematic situations. This, in turn, will permit more formal testing, application, and subsequent modification of the theory of face management in close relationships.

ᴥ Implications of Face Management

Relational Culture and Face

The theory of face management highlights some important features in the conduct of close relationships. Chief among these is the idea that relational partners co-construct the interaction episodes that constitute their relationship. Face is not merely what one individual dictates. Rather, partners negotiate (usually tacitly) who each other "is" with respect to one another. Each partner contributes to defining the identity that is expected to be displayed when they interact and normally reach what Goffman calls a "working consensus" with regard to the face and behavioral line that each is expected to assume in particular encounters. As a meaningful relationship develops, the working consensus evolves into a relational culture that encompasses both partners and spans their interactions with one another. This culture is fluid and amorphous, but contextualizes the meanings that each partner draws from his or her interactions.

Face and the Dialectical Nature of Relationships

Another important feature emphasized by face management theory is the dialectical nature of the formation (and erosion) of relationships. By nature, relationships are paradoxical. They are filled with dilemmas and contradictions. The most fundamental contradiction of all that individuals must manage in relationships is the inherent tension between autonomy and interdependence that attends the development of a close relationship (e.g., Baxter, 1988, 1990; Goldsmith, 1990). These simultaneous but opposing tendencies are tantamount to negative and positive face needs, respectively. Managing a relationship with another entails the management of one's own conflicting desires for both independence and connectedness.

Simultaneously maintaining both one's own face and a partner's face also poses a dialectical conflict for each partner in a relationship. One's own face must be supported if one is to possess the virtues of pride, dignity, and self-esteem; but one's partner's face must be supported if the partner is to possess these virtues. To the extent there is mutual face support, a stable relationship between partners is possible. Each partner counts on the other to support the partner's face cooperatively—"I'll scratch your back and you scratch mine; I'll anoint your face and you anoint mine." Of course, this principle underlies all social interaction to an extent. There is always the expectation that individuals should demonstrate self-respect and considerateness to others. As relationships grow in intimacy, partners presumably work harder to enhance their partners' face and demonstrate respect for their partners at more profound levels. Enhancing one's partner's face works to the extent that supporting partner's face is compatible with one's own face needs—that is, supporting partner and the relationship is seen as producing support for self. When relationships break down or dissolve, one or both partners exhibit a competitive orientation in which one's own face takes precedence over the partner's. However, even in the face of a disintegrating relationship, partners can assist each other in saving face.

Intimacy and Facework

The escalation of intimacy in relationships parallels the development of familiarity between partners and feelings of closeness or attachment. We might assume, therefore, that as relationships become more intimate, partners are more attentive to each other's face needs. Several studies have shown, for example, that politeness efforts are greater in closer relationships compared with distant relationships (Baxter, 1984; Leichty & Applegate, 1991; Lim & Bowers, 1991). Certainly when the goal is to increase intimacy and closeness in a relationship, an individual tries to put on his or her best "face" to make a good impression. That means the person attempts to appear competent, likable, trustworthy, and so on. It also means that he or she will ingratiate the partner by giving compliments, avoiding disagreements, emphasizing things in common, and so forth. At a general level, the development of intimacy in relationships is grounded heavily in the mutual support of positive face. Each partner bolsters solidarity of the relationship by communicating liking, respect, and similarity.

Of course, when a relationship has achieved a high degree of intimacy, efforts to support the positive face of a partner may not be as regular or as obvious. In established relationships, support for positive face is *assumed*. The existence of the relationship implies that positive face is supported and is reciprocated over time. Each and every conversation need not demonstrate overt efforts to support partner's positive face. Because the relationship has systematically accumulated face support, it needs periodic maintenance or reinforcement rather than the constant overt attention that was displayed when partners were trying to create intimacy and a joint identity. As a consequence of the developed relational culture, some acts that were once seen as threatening to positive face are now not taken to be face-threatening.

Part of the nature of close relationships is the expectation that partners can rely on one another. As Michael Roloff and his colleagues have demonstrated, intimacy entails sensitivity to the partner's needs for assistance and the tendency to oblige (see, e.g., Roloff & Janiszewski, 1989; Roloff, Janiszewski, McGrath, Burns, & Manrai, 1988). It is simply the essence of close relationships that some degree of autonomy is voluntarily sacrificed for the sake of intimacy. Close relationships are marked by relatively more openness and frankness and relatively less tact and circumscription than are distant relationships. Moreover, close relationships have the opportunity to develop a "thick skin." That is, the bonds of solidarity impart a certain resilience to the relationship, allowing it to more easily withstand threats to negative face that would not be tolerated from another person. Thus overt negative politeness tends to decrease as relationships become more intimate (Brown & Levinson, 1987; Lim, 1990).

But maintaining face is a concern in all relationships. It is not simply the case that intimate relationships always entail more politeness or always exhibit less tact. The connection between intimacy and facework is more complex than that. It is likely, for instance, that the level of intimacy in a relationship influences what a person considers to be face-threatening as well as the degree of face threat attached to a specific behavior. Because partners acquire intimate knowledge about one another as a relationship grows, they gain specific information regarding what each other finds particularly face-threatening or face-enhancing.

The effect of intimacy on face redress also depends on the degree of face threat implied in an act (Leichty & Applegate, 1991; Lim & Bowers, 1991). Thus, in situations that would normally involve only a modicum of face threat, intimates require less attention to positive and negative face compared with nonintimates. Requesting a small favor from an acquaintance creates more of an imposition than does making the same request of a spouse. Hence less politeness is needed or exhibited with the spouse because there is little implied face threat. However, when an act constitutes an extraordinary imposition on the partner, it implies a sort of "disrespect" or "disregard" for the relationship. When behavior threatens the mutually accepted definition of the relationship, the obligation to redress partner's face is greater in intimate versus nonintimate relationships. To berate a coworker for doing something stupid threatens the coworker's face; to berate a lover for doing something stupid *smashes* the lover's face.

Relational Culture and the Social Network

The development of a co-constructed relational culture suggests that partners' individual identities become interdependent and enmeshed. Consequently, the partners share and present a joint "relational face" when interacting with other people. When two individuals are seen by their social network as a "couple," then the dyadic relationship is ascribed an identity, just as each individual is. Consequently, relational partners receive joint gifts and joint invitations, and network members perceive characteristics about the couple as well as about the individuals constituting the couple. Steve and Sherry, as a couple, may be seen by their "couple friends" as committed, socially active, private about their relationship, and so forth (whereas Steve is seen as reserved and competitive, and Sherry is seen as friendly, witty, and so on).

Similarly, Steve and Sherry individually and collectively put up a relational "front" when interacting with members of their families and social networks. They may present the image (true or not) that their relationship is relatively conflict free and that they are completely open with one another. Of course, the relational image presented to one person or group deliberately may be different from the image presented to another. But the point is that close relationships have a sort of relational face to which partners are tied that is presented to others for validation. Naturally, a problematic situation occurs when members of a social network do not support the relational face presented by partners. If Jennifer, one of Sherry's friends, challenges the image of Sherry and Steve's relationship, she threatens Sherry and Steve's relationship as well as Jennifer and Sherry's.

Perhaps more problematic is the situation in which one partner publicly disconfirms the mutually agreed-on public definition of the relationship. If Steve and Sherry are having a spat while also attending a party, Steve may lose his temper and thereby threaten the face that Steve and Sherry normally present. Sherry naturally resents this because to threaten the public face of the relationship is also to threaten Sherry's individual face, which is inherently tied to the relational face. Steve's individual face has been threatened too, though he has done so deliberately in an aggressive attempt to threaten Sherry's face during their interpersonal conflict. Whether intentional or inadvertent, when one partner disconfirms or threatens the mutually constructed relationship face, he or she is also threatening the face of the individual relational partners.

Problematic Episodes

The selection of relationship phenomena we have elaborated in this book is representative rather than exhaustive. Certainly, other problematic episodes in close relationships deserve scrutiny under the lens of face theory. Given that a comprehensive delineation of such episodes is not currently available, one agenda for future research is to develop a taxonomy of problematic situations in relationships. Michael Motley (1992) has recently identified a preliminary list of problematic communication situations by analyzing Dear-Abby-type letters solicited from undergraduate students. The particularly problematic situations include the following:

> (a) communicating safe-sex expectations in the first sexual episode with a given partner . . . , (b) communicating the desire to escalate the emotional intensity of a relationship, (c) communicating the desire to terminate or deescalate a relationship, (d) initiating conversation with a receiver to whom the sender is attracted, (e) discovering the extent to which one's views of a relationship are mutual, (f) maintaining or reestablishing relationships while resolving conflicts that have reached competitive win-lose levels, (g) disclosure of strong emotions and attitudes (positive or negative) in established relationships, (h) tactful assertiveness to relationally valued receivers of views perceived as unfavorable to them, (i) negotiating behavioral or attitudinal independence from parents . . . , (j) advising

others to seek professional help for apparent disorders (e.g., alcohol, gambling, depression). (p. 308)

Although Motley's research was reported after we organized the topics to cover in this book, we have touched on most of the situations he identifies. Certainly, additional research on other populations is warranted if we are to get the complete picture.

Interpersonal Competence, Relational Compatibility, and Face

Just as individuals differ in their personal orientations to relationships, we might speculate that individuals also differ in their relative levels of face needs. Some people have greater need for autonomy and freedom in their relationships compared with other people. Certain individuals require greater amounts of approval and acceptance compared with others. These individual differences are manifested in communication behavior and ultimately affect the extent to which partners find interaction with each other enjoyable.

Individuals also exhibit differences with respect to their motivation and ability to address the face needs of others (e.g., Hale, 1986; Leichty & Applegate, 1991; O'Keefe, 1988). Recall from Chapter 1 that interpersonal competence entails effectively managing face concerns. Discrepancies in the face needs exhibited by one partner and the face attention offered by the other are likely to affect the long-term viability and stability of the relationship. Differences in the face needs and face-giving proclivities of individual partners affect their compatibility. If Cindy has a high need for autonomy in her relationship with Alex, the stability of the relationship will be threatened if Alex is disinclined to respect Cindy's autonomy. Unless Cindy reduces her need for autonomy or Alex grants her more autonomy, the discrepancy will cause Cindy to be dissatisfied with her relationship to Alex, and it will remain a potential source of interpersonal conflict between them. If Rodney has strong needs for signs of affiliation and positive regard from his partner, Wendy, and if Wendy fulfills those needs, it should be a source of satisfaction for Rodney and should contribute to the stability of his relationship with Wendy. Thus correspondence between relational partners on aspects of face needs should provide an indication of relational compatibility. To the extent that partners exhibit complementarity in their desire for and attention to face wants, positive individual and relational outcomes should accrue (Cupach & Metts, 1993).

Facework in Intercultural Relationships

People in all cultures presumably present identities through face and share the motive to maintain face (Brown & Levinson, 1987; Tracy, 1990). However, cultural members differ from one another in the implementation and interpretation of facework. Cultures differ with respect to the relative value placed on different face needs, the behaviors that are seen as face-threatening and face-supporting, and the behaviors that are preferred to minimize or repair face threats (Collier, 1989; Matsumoto, 1988; Scollon & Scollon, 1981; Sueda & Wiseman, 1992; Ting-Toomey, 1988). Consequently, the development of intercultural relationships (i.e., close relationships between individuals from two different cultures) can be particularly problematic. Intercultural partners inevitably must negotiate their respective orientations to face if they are to develop an intimate relationship. Research regarding the processes of face management in intercultural couples can provide insight into how intercultural partners overcome the cultural barriers that can undermine the formation of a successful close relationship. Thus face management theory may be uniquely suited for exploring the negotiation and development of "intercultural" and "interethnic" relationships (Cupach & Imahori, 1993a).

✿ Conclusion

Erving Goffman (1967) has argued that people in all societies are "taught to be perceptive, to have feelings attached to self and a self expressed through face, to have pride, honor, and dignity, to have considerateness, to have tact and a certain amount of poise"

(p. 44). To that extent, the concepts of face and facework seem to be particularly powerful tools for gaining insight into the conduct and experience of human relationships. We have only chipped the surface of a rather large iceberg in this book. Problematic situations in relationships are only part of the broader picture, albeit an essential part in our view. Our analysis of face issues is representative rather than comprehensive and heuristic rather than definitive at this point. Face management theory needs further articulation and formalization to reach its full potential. Our hope is that further elaboration and appropriate testing of the theory will ultimately lead to a more complete understanding about competent interpersonal communicators and successful close relationships.

References

Abbey, A. (1982). Sex differences in attributions for friendly behavior: Do males misperceive females' friendliness? *Journal of Personality and Social Psychology, 42,* 830-838.

Abbey, A., & Melby, C. (1986). The effects of nonverbal cues on gender differences in perceptions of sexual intent. *Sex Roles, 15,* 283-298.

Adelman, M. B. (1991). Play and incongruity: Framing safe-sex talk. *Health Communication, 3,* 139-155.

Adelman, M. B. (1992). Healthy passions: Safer sex as play. In T. Edgar, M. A. Fitzpatrick, & V. S. Freimuth (Eds.), *AIDS: A communication perspective* (pp. 69-89). Hillsdale, NJ: Lawrence Erlbaum.

Alberts, J. K. (1988). An analysis of couples' conversational complaints. *Communication Monographs, 55,* 184-197.

Alberts, J. K. (1989). A descriptive taxonomy of couples' complaint interactions. *Southern Communication Journal, 54,* 125-143.

Alberts, J. K., & Driscoll, G. (1992). Containment versus escalation: The trajectory of couples' conversation complaints. *Western Journal of Communication, 56,* 394-412.

Argyle, M., Furnham, A., & Graham, J. A. (1981). *Social situations*. Cambridge: Cambridge University Press.

Arnold, C. L., & Honska, J. R. (1992, November). *Reducing interpersonal embarrassment in sexual situations: Testing an eight strategy approach.* Paper presented at the annual meeting of the Speech Communication Association, Chicago.

Askham, J. (1976). Identity and stability within the marriage relationship. *Journal of Marriage and the Family, 38*, 535-547.

Banks, S. P., Altendorf, D. M., Greene, J. O., & Cody, M. J. (1987). An examination of relationship disengagement: Perceptions, breakup strategies and outcomes. *Western Journal of Speech Communication, 51*, 19-41.

Barrera, M., Jr., & Ainlay, S. L. (1983). The structure of social support: A conceptual and empirical analysis. *Journal of Community Psychology, 11*, 133-143.

Baxter, L. A. (1982). Strategies for ending relationships: Two studies. *Western Journal of Speech Communication, 51*, 19-41.

Baxter, L. A. (1984). An investigation of compliance-gaining as politeness. *Human Communication Research, 10*, 427-456.

Baxter, L. A. (1985). Accomplishing relationship disengagement. In S. Duck & D. Perlman (Eds.), *Understanding personal relationships* (pp. 243-265). London: Sage.

Baxter, L. A. (1987). Cognition and communication in the relationship process. In R. Burnett, P. McGhee, & D. D. Clarke (Eds.), *Accounting for relationships* (pp. 192-212). London: Methuen.

Baxter, L. A. (1988). A dialectical perspective on communication strategies in relationship development. In S. Duck (Ed.), *Handbook of personal relationships: Theory, research, interventions* (pp. 257-273). London: John Wiley.

Baxter, L. A. (1990). Dialectical contradictions in relationship development. *Journal of Social and Personal Relationships, 7*, 69-88.

Baxter, L. A. (1992). Forms and functions of intimate play in personal relationships. *Human Communication Research, 18*, 336-363.

Bell, R. A., Buerkel-Rothfuss, N. L., & Gore, K. E. (1987). "Did you bring the yarmulke for the Cabbage Patch kid?": The idiomatic communication of young lovers. *Human Communication Research, 14*, 47-67.

Bell, R. A., & Daly, J. A. (1984). The affinity-seeking function of communication. *Communication Monographs, 51*, 91-115.

Bell, R. A., & Healey, J. G. (1992). Idiomatic communication and interpersonal solidarity in friends' relational cultures. *Human Communication Research, 18*, 307-335.

Berger, C. R. (1979). Beyond initial interaction: Uncertainty, understanding, and the development of interpersonal relationships. In H. Giles & R. N. St. Clair (Eds.), *Language and social psychology* (pp. 122-144). Baltimore: University Park Press.

Berger, C. R., & Bradac, J. J. (1982). *Language and social knowledge.* Baltimore: Edward Arnold.

Berger, C. R., & Calabrese, R. J. (1975). Some explorations in initial interaction and beyond: Toward a developmental theory of interpersonal communication. *Human Communication Research, 1,* 99-112.

Betcher, R. W. (1981). Intimate play and marital adaptation. *Psychiatry, 44,* 13-33.

Blumstein, P. W., Carssow, K. G., Hall, J., Hawkins, B., Hoffman, R., Ishem, E., Maurer, C. P., Spens, D., Taylor, J., & Zimmerman, D. L. (1974). The honoring of accounts. *American Sociological Review, 39,* 551-566.

Brehm, S. S. (1985). *Intimate relationships.* New York: Random House.

Brenton, M. (1973). *Sex talk.* London: Allison & Busby.

Brown, B. R. (1970). Face-saving following experimentally induced embarrassment. *Journal of Experimental Social Psychology, 6,* 255-271.

Brown, M., & Auerback, A. (1981). Communication patterns in initiation of marital sex. *Medical Aspects of Human Sexuality, 15,* 107-117.

Brown, P., & Levinson, S. (1987). *Politeness: Some universals in language usage.* Cambridge: Cambridge University Press.

Burleson, B. R. (1990). Comforting as social support: Relational consequences of supportive behaviors. In S. Duck (Ed.), *Personal relationships and social support* (pp. 66-82). London: Sage.

Burleson, B. R., & Denton, W. H. (1992). A new look at similarity and attraction in marriage: Similarities in social-cognitive and communication skills as predictors of attraction and satisfaction. *Communication Monographs, 59,* 268-287.

Buss, A. H. (1980). *Self-consciousness and social anxiety.* San Francisco: W. H. Freeman.

Buttny, R. (1985). Accounts as a reconstruction of an event's context. *Communication Monographs, 52,* 57-77.

Buttny, R. (1987). Sequence and practical reasoning in accounts episodes. *Communication Quarterly, 35,* 67-83.

Buunk, B., & Bringle, R. G. (1987). Jealousy in love relationships. In D. Perlman & S. Duck (Eds.), *Intimate relationships: Development, dynamics, and deterioration* (pp. 123-147). Newbury Park, CA: Sage.

Byers, E. S. (1988). Effects of sexual arousal on men's and women's behavior in sexual disagreement situations. *Journal of Sex Research, 25,* 235-254.

Byers, E. S., & Heinlein, L. (1989). Predicting initiations and refusals of sexual activities in married and cohabiting heterosexual couples. *Journal of Sex Research, 26,* 210-231.

Byrne, D. (1971). *The attraction paradigm.* New York: Academic Press.

Castelfranchi, C., & Poggi, I. (1990). Blushing as discourse: Was Darwin wrong? In W. R. Crozier (Ed.), *Shyness and embarrassment: Perspectives from social psychology* (pp. 230-251). Cambridge: Cambridge University Press.

Christopher, F. S., & Frandsen, M. M. (1990). Strategies of influence in sex and dating. *Journal of Social and Personal Relationships, 7*, 89-105.

Cline, R. J., Johnson, S. J., & Freeman, K. E. (1992). Talk among sexual partners: Interpersonal communication for risk reduction or risk enhancement. *Health Communication, 4*, 39-56.

Cody, M. J. (1982). A typology of disengagement strategies and an examination of the role intimacy, reactions to inequity and relational problems play in strategy selection. *Communication Monographs, 49*, 148-170.

Cody, M. J., & McLaughlin, M. L. (1985). Models for the sequential construction of accounting episodes: Situational and interactional constraints on message selection and evaluation. In R. L. Street & J. N. Cappella (Eds.), *Sequence and pattern in communicative behavior* (pp. 50-69). Baltimore: Edward Arnold.

Collier, M. J. (1989). Cultural and intercultural communication competence: Current approaches and directions for future research. *International Journal of Intercultural Relations, 13*, 287-302.

Coyne, J. C., & De Longis, A. (1986). Going beyond social support: The role of social relationships in adaptation. *Journal of Consulting and Clinical Psychology, 54*, 454-460.

Coyne, J. C., Ellard, J. H., & Smith, D. A. F. (1990). Social support, interdependence, and the dilemmas of helping. In B. R. Sarason, I. G. Sarason, & G. R. Pierce (Eds.), *Social support: An interactional view* (pp. 129-149). New York: John Wiley.

Cupach, W. R., & Imahori, T. T. (1993a). Identity management theory: Communication competence in intercultural episodes and relationships. In R. L. Wiseman & J. Koester (Eds.), *Intercultural communication competence* (pp. 112-131). Newbury Park, CA: Sage.

Cupach, W. R., & Imahori, T. T. (1993b). Managing social predicaments created by others: A comparison of Japanese and American facework. *Western Journal of Communication, 57*, 431-444.

Cupach, W. R., & Metts, S. (1990). Remedial processes in embarrassing predicaments. In J. A. Anderson (Ed.), *Communication yearbook 13* (pp. 323-352). Newbury Park, CA: Sage.

Cupach, W. R., & Metts, S. (1991). Sexuality and communication in close relationships. In K. McKinney & S. Sprecher (Eds.), *Sexuality in close relationships* (pp. 93-110). Hillsdale, NJ: Lawrence Erlbaum.

Cupach, W. R., & Metts, S. (1992). The effects of type of predicament and embarrassability on remedial responses to embarrassing situations. *Communication Quarterly, 40*, 149-161.

Cupach, W. R., & Metts, S. (1993, June). *Correspondence between relationship partners on relationship beliefs and face predilections as predictors of rela-*

tional quality. Paper presented at the conference of the International Network on Personal Relationships, Milwaukee, WI.

Cupach, W. R., Metts, S., & Hazleton, V. (1986). Coping with embarrassing predicaments: Remedial strategies and their perceived utility. *Journal of Language and Social Psychology, 5,* 181-200.

Cutrona, C. E., Suhr, J. A., & MacFarlane, R. (1990). Interpersonal transactions and the psychological sense of support. In S. Duck (Ed.), *Personal relationships and social support* (pp. 30-45). London: Sage.

Darby, B. W., & Schlenker, B. R. (1982). Children's reactions to apologies. *Journal of Personality and Social Psychology, 43,* 742-753.

Darby, B. W., & Schlenker, B. R. (1989). Children's reactions to transgressions: Effects of the actor's apology, reputation and remorse. *British Journal of Social Psychology, 28,* 353-364.

Douglas, W. (1987). Affinity-testing in initial interaction. *Journal of Social and Personal Relationships, 4,* 3-16.

Edelmann, R. J. (1982). The effect of embarrassed reactions upon others. *Australian Journal of Psychology, 34,* 359-367.

Edelmann, R. J. (1985). Social embarrassment: An analysis of the process. *Journal of Social and Personal Relationships, 2,* 195-213.

Edelmann, R. J. (1987). *The psychology of embarrassment.* Chichester, UK: John Wiley.

Edgar, T., & Fitzpatrick, M. A. (1988). Compliance-gaining in relational interaction: When your life depends on it. *Southern Speech Communication Journal, 53,* 385-405.

Edgar, T., & Fitzpatrick, M. A. (1990). Communicating sexual desire: Message tactics for having and avoiding intercourse. In J. P. Dillard (Ed.), *Seeking compliance: The production of interpersonal influence messages* (pp. 107-121). Scottsdale, AZ: Gorsuch Scarisbrick.

Ellis, C., & Weinstein, E. (1986). Jealousy and the social psychology of emotional experience. *Journal of Social and Personal Relationships, 3,* 337-357.

Falbo, T., & Peplau, L. A. (1980). Power strategies in intimate relationships. *Journal of Personality and Social Psychology, 38,* 618-628.

Fincham, F. D. (1992). The account episode in close relationships. In M. L. McLaughlin, M. J. Cody, & S. J. Read (Eds.), *Explaining one's self to others: Reason-giving in a social context* (pp. 167-182). Hillsdale, NJ: Lawrence Erlbaum.

Fink, E. L., & Walker, B. A. (1977). Humorous responses to embarrassment. *Psychological Reports, 40,* 475-485.

Fletcher, G. J. O., & Kininmonth, L. A. (1992). Measuring relationship beliefs: An individual differences scale. *Journal of Research in Personality, 26,* 371-397.

Fraser, B. (1981). On apologizing. In F. Coulmas (Ed.), *Conversational routine: Explorations in standardized communication situations and prepatterned speech* (pp. 259-271). New York: Mouton.

Glidewell, J. C., Tucker, S., Todt, M., & Cox, S. (1983). Professional support systems: The teaching profession. In A. Nadler, J. D. Fisher, & B. M. DePaulo (Eds.), *New directions in helping: Vol. 3. Applied perspectives on help-seeking and receiving* (pp. 189-212). New York: Academic Press.

Goffman, E. (1959). *The presentation of self in everyday life.* New York: Overlook.

Goffman, E. (1967). *Interaction ritual: Essays on face-to-face behavior.* New York: Pantheon.

Goffman, E. (1971). *Relations in public.* New York: Basic Books.

Goldsmith, D. (1990). A dialectic perspective on the expression of autonomy and connection in romantic relationships. *Western Journal of Speech Communication, 54,* 537-556.

Goldsmith, D. (1992). Managing conflicting goals in supportive interaction: An integrative theoretical framework. *Communication Research, 19,* 264-286.

Goldsmith, D., & Parks, M. R. (1990). Communicative strategies for managing the risks of seeking social support. In S. Duck (Ed.), *Personal relationships and social support* (pp. 104-121). London: Sage.

Gonzales, M. H., Pederson, J. H., Manning, D. J., & Wetter, D. W. (1991). Pardon my gaffe: Effects of sex, status, and consequence severity on accounts. *Journal of Personality and Social Psychology, 58,* 610-621.

Gottman, J. M. (1979). *Marital interaction: Experimental investigations.* New York: Academic Press.

Gottman, J. M. (1982). Emotional responsiveness in marital conversations. *Journal of Communication, 32,* 108-120.

Gross, E., & Stone, G. P. (1964). Embarrassment and the analysis of role requirements. *American Journal of Sociology, 70,* 1-15.

Hale, C. L. (1986). The impact of cognitive complexity on message structure in a face-threatening context. *Journal of Language and Social Psychology, 5,* 135-143.

Hale, C. L. (1987). A comparison of accounts: When is a failure not a failure? *Journal of Language and Social Psychology, 6,* 117-132.

Harris, T. E. (1984). The "faux pas" in interpersonal communication. In S. Thomas (Ed.), *Communication theory and interpersonal interaction* (pp. 53-61). Norwood, NJ: Ablex.

Hewitt, J., & Stokes, R. (1975). Disclaimers. *American Sociological Review, 40,* 1-11.

Ho, D. Y. F. (1976). On the concept of face. *American Journal of Sociology, 81,* 867-884.

Holtgraves, T. (1989). The form and function of remedial moves: Reported use, psychological reality and perceived effectiveness. *Journal of Language and Social Psychology, 8,* 1-16.

Honska, J. R., & Arnold, C. L. (1992, May). *Reducing the interpersonal embarrassment in a sexual context: A new typology.* Paper presented at the annual meeting of the International Communication Association, Miami, FL.

Hopper, R., Knapp, M. L., & Scott, L. (1981). Couples' personal idioms: Exploring intimate talk. *Journal of Communication, 31,* 23-33.

Imahori, T. T., & Cupach, W. R. (1991, March). *A cross-cultural comparison of the interpretation and management of face: American and Japanese responses to embarrassing predicaments.* Paper presented at the Conference on Communication in Japan and the United States, California State University, Fullerton.

Knapp, M. L., Stafford, L., & Daly, J. (1986). Regrettable messages: Things people wish they hadn't said. *Journal of Communication, 36,* 40-58.

Knapp, M. L., & Vangelisti, A. (1992). *Interpersonal communication and human relationships.* Boston: Allyn & Bacon.

Labov, W., & Fanshel, D. (1977). *Therapeutic discourse: Psychotherapy as conversation.* New York: Academic Press.

La Gaipa, J. J. (1990). The negative effects of informal support systems. In S. Duck (Ed.), *Personal relationships and social support* (pp. 122-139). London: Sage.

LaPlante, M. N., McCormick, N., & Brannigan, G. G. (1980). Living the sexual script: College students' views of influence in sexual encounters. *Journal of Sex Research, 16,* 338-355.

Leary, M. R., & Meadows, S. (1991). Predictors, elicitors, and concomitants of social blushing. *Journal of Personality and Social Psychology, 60,* 254-262.

Leichty, G., & Applegate, J. L. (1991). Social-cognitive and situational influences on the use of face-saving persuasive strategies. *Human Communication Research, 17,* 451-484.

Levin, J., & Arluke, A. (1982). Embarrassment and helping behavior. *Psychological Reports, 51,* 999-1002.

Lim, T. S. (1990). Politeness behavior in social influence situations. In J. P. Dillard (Ed.), *Seeking compliance: The production of interpersonal influence messages* (pp. 75-86). Scottsdale, AZ: Gorsuch Scarisbrick.

Lim, T. S., & Bowers, J. W. (1991). Facework: Solidarity, approbation, and tact. *Human Communication Research, 17,* 415-450.

Lock, A. J. (1986). The role of relationships in development: An introduction to a series of occasional articles. *Journal of Social and Personal Relationships, 3,* 89-100.

Matsumoto, Y. (1988). Reexamination of the universality of face: Politeness phenomena in Japanese. *Journal of Pragmatics, 12,* 403-426.

McCormick, N. B. (1979). Come-ons and put-offs: Unmarried students' strategies for having and avoiding sexual intercourse. *Psychology of Women Quarterly, 4,* 194-211.

McLaughlin, M. L., Cody, M. J., & O'Hair, H. D. (1983). The management of failure events: Some contextual determinants of accounting behavior. *Human Communication Research, 9,* 208-224.

Metts, S. (1991, February). *Coping with relational transgressions.* Paper presented at the annual meeting of the Western Communication Association, Phoenix, AZ.

Metts, S. (1992). The language of disengagement: A face-management perspective. In T. L. Orbuch (Ed.), *Close relationship loss: Theoretical approaches* (pp. 111-127). New York: Springer-Verlag.

Metts, S., Aune, K., & Ebesu, A. (1990, February). *Managing the discovery of deception.* Paper presented at the annual meeting of the Western Communication Association, Sacramento, CA.

Metts, S., & Cupach, W. R. (1989a). The role of communication in human sexuality. In K. McKinney & S. Sprecher (Eds.), *Human sexuality: The societal and interpersonal context* (pp. 139-161). Norwood, NJ: Ablex.

Metts, S., & Cupach, W. R. (1989b). Situational influence on the use of remedial strategies in embarrassing predicaments. *Communication Monographs, 56,* 151-162.

Metts, S., Cupach, W. R., & Bejlovec, R. (1989). "I love you too much to ever stop liking you": Redefining romantic relationships. *Journal of Social and Personal Relationships, 6,* 259-274.

Metts, S., Cupach, W. R., & Imahori, T. T. (1992). Perceptions of sexual compliance-resisting messages in three types of cross-sex relationships. *Western Journal of Communication, 56,* 1-17.

Metts, S., & Mongeau, P. (1991, November). *The management of critical events in continuing and noncontinuing relationships.* Paper presented at the annual meeting of the Speech Communication Association, Atlanta, GA.

Miller, R. S. (1986). Embarrassment: Causes and consequences. In W. H. Jones, J. M. Cheek, & S. R. Briggs (Eds.), *Shyness: Perspectives on research and treatment* (pp. 295-311). New York: Plenum.

Miller, R. S. (1987). Empathic embarrassment: Situational and personal determinants of reactions to the embarrassment of another. *Journal of Personality and Social Psychology, 53,* 1061-1069.

Miller, R. S. (1992). The nature and severity of self-reported embarrassing circumstances. *Personality and Social Psychology Bulletin, 18,* 190-198.

Miller, R. S., & Leary, M. R. (1992). Social sources and interactive functions of emotion: The case of embarrassment. In M. S. Clark (Ed.), *Emotion and social behavior* (pp. 202-221). Newbury Park, CA: Sage.

Modigliani, A. (1968). Embarrassment and embarrassability. *Sociometry, 31,* 313-326.

Modigliani, A. (1971). Embarrassment, facework, and eye contact: Testing a theory of embarrassment. *Journal of Personality and Social Psychology, 17,* 15-24.

Moore, M. M. (1985). Nonverbal courtship patterns in women: Context and consequences. *Ethology and Sociobiology, 6,* 237-247.

Motley, M. T. (1992). Mindfulness in solving communicators' dilemmas. *Communication Monographs, 59,* 306-314.

Muehlenhard, C. L., & Hollabaugh, L. C. (1988). Do women sometimes say no when they mean yes? The prevalence and correlates of women's token resistance to sex. *Journal of Personality and Social Psychology, 54,* 872-879.

Muehlenhard, C. L., & Linton, M. (1987). Date rape and sexual aggression in dating situations: Incidence and risk factors. *Journal of Counseling Psychology, 34,* 186-196.

Murnen, S. K., Perot, A., & Byrne, D. (1989). Coping with unwanted sexual activity: Normative responses, situational determinants, and individual differences. *Journal of Sex Research, 26,* 85-106.

Ohbuchi, K., Kameda, M., & Agarie, N. (1989). Apology as aggression control: Its role in mediating appraisal of and response to harm. *Journal of Personality and Social Psychology, 56,* 219-227.

O'Keefe, B. J. (1988). The logic of message design: Individual differences in reasoning about communication. *Communication Monographs, 55,* 80-103.

Penman, R. (1990). Facework and politeness: Multiple goals in courtroom discourse. *Journal of Language and Social Psychology, 9,* 15-38.

Peplau, L. A., Rubin, Z., & Hill, C. T. (1977). Sexual intimacy in dating relationships. *Journal of Social Issues, 33,* 86-109.

Perper, T., & Weis, D. L. (1987). Proceptive and rejective strategies of U.S. and Canadian college women. *Journal of Sex Research, 23,* 455-480.

Petronio, S. (1984). Communication strategies to reduce embarrassment: Differences between men and women. *Western Journal of Speech Communication, 48,* 28-38.

Petronio, S., Olson, C., & Dollar, N. (1988). Relational embarrassment: Impact on relational quality and communication satisfaction. In H. D. O'Hair & B. R. Patterson (Eds.), *Advances in interpersonal communication research* (Proceedings of the Western Speech Communication Association Interpersonal Communication Interest Group) (pp. 195-206). Las Cruces: New Mexico State University, Communication Resources Center.

Procidano, M. E., & Heller, K. (1983). Measures of perceived support from friends and from family: Three validation studies. *American Journal of Community Psychology, 11,* 1-24.

Roloff, M. E., & Cloven, D. H. (1990). The chilling effect in interpersonal relationships: The reluctance to speak one's mind. In D. D. Cahn (Ed.), *Intimates in conflict: A communication perspective* (pp. 49-76). Hillsdale, NJ: Lawrence Erlbaum.

Roloff, M. E., & Janiszewski, C. A. (1989). Overcoming obstacles to interpersonal compliance: A principle of message construction. *Human Communication Research, 16,* 33-61.

Roloff, M. E., Janiszewski, C. A., McGrath, M. A., Burns, C. S., & Manrai, L. A. (1988). Acquiring resources from intimates: When obligation substitutes for persuasion. *Human Communication Research, 14,* 364-396.

Rook, K. S. (1985). The functions of social bonds: Perspectives from research on social support, loneliness, and social isolation. In I. G. Sarason & B. R. Sarason (Eds.), *Social support: Theory, research and applications* (pp. 243-268). The Hague: Martinus Nijhoff.

Sarason, I. G., Levine, H. M., Basham, R. B., & Sarason, B. R. (1983). Assessing social support: The Social Support Questionnaire. *Journal of Personality and Social Psychology, 44,* 127-139.

Sattler, J. M. (1965). A theoretical, developmental, and clinical investigation of embarrassment. *Genetic Psychology Monographs, 71,* 19-59.

Schlenker, B. R. (1980). *Impression management: The self-concept, social identity, and interpersonal relations.* Monterey, CA: Brooks/Cole.

Schlenker, B. R., & Darby, B. W. (1981). The use of apologies in social predicaments. *Social Psychology Quarterly, 44,* 271- 278.

Schonbach, P. (1980). A category system for account phases. *European Journal of Social Psychology, 10,* 195-200.

Schonbach, P. (1990). *Account episodes: The management or escalation of conflict.* Cambridge: Cambridge University Press.

Scollon, R., & Scollon, S. (1981). *Narrative, literacy and face in interethnic communication.* Norwood, NJ: Ablex.

Scott, M. B., & Lyman, S. M. (1968). Accounts. *American Sociological Review, 33,* 46-62.

Semin, G. R., & Manstead, A. S. R. (1982). The social implications of embarrassment displays and restitution behavior. *European Journal of Social Psychology, 12,* 367-377.

Semin, G. R., & Manstead, A. S. R. (1983). *The accountability of conduct: A social psychological analysis.* London: Academic Press.

Semin, G. R., & Papadopoulou, K. (1990). The acquisition of reflexive social emotions: The transmission and reproduction of social control through joint action. In G. Duveen & B. Lloyd (Eds.), *Social representations and the development of knowledge* (pp. 107-125). Cambridge: Cambridge University Press.

Sharkey, W. F. (1991). Intentional embarrassment: Goals, tactics, and consequences. In W. R. Cupach & S. Metts (Eds.), *Advances in interpersonal communication research, 1991* (Proceedings of the Western Speech Communication Association Interpersonal Communication Interest Group) (pp. 105-128). Normal: Illinois State University, Personal Relationships Research Group.

Sharkey, W. F. (1993). Who embarrasses whom? Relational and sex differences in the use of intentional embarrassment. In P. J. Kalbfleisch (Ed.), *Interpersonal communication: Evolving interpersonal relationships* (pp. 147-168). Hillsdale, NJ: Lawrence Erlbaum.

Sharkey, W. F., & Stafford, L. (1988, November). *I've never been so embarrassed: Degree of embarrassment and its effect upon communicative responses.* Paper presented at the annual meeting of the Speech Communication Association, New Orleans.

Sharkey, W. F., & Stafford, L. (1990). Responses to embarrassment. *Human Communication Research, 17,* 315-342.

Shimanoff, S. B. (1985). Rules governing the verbal expression of emotions between married couples. *Western Journal of Speech Communication, 49,* 147-165.

Shimanoff, S. B. (1987). Types of emotional disclosures and request compliance between spouses. *Communication Monographs, 54,* 85-100.

Shotland, R. L., & Craig, J. M. (1988). Can men and women differentiate between friendly and sexually interested behavior? *Social Psychology Quarterly, 51,* 66-73.

Silver, M., Sabini, J., & Parrott, W. G. (1987). Embarrassment: A dramaturgic account. *Journal for the Theory of Social Behaviour, 17,* 47-61.

Snyder, C. R. (1985). The excuse: An amazing grace? In B. R. Schlenker (Ed.), *The self and social life* (pp. 235-260). New York: McGraw-Hill.

Snyder, C. R., & Higgins, R. L. (1988). Excuses: Their effective role in the negotiation of reality. *Psychological Bulletin, 104,* 23-35.

Snyder, C. R., & Higgins, R. L. (1990). Reality negotiation and excuse-making: President Reagan's 4 March 1987 Iran arms scandal speech and other literature. In M. J. Cody & M. L. McLaughlin (Eds.), *The psychology of tactical communication* (pp. 207-228). Clevedon, England: Multilingual Matters.

Snyder, C. R., Higgins, R. L., & Stuckey, R. J. (1983). *Excuses: Masquerades in search of grace.* New York: John Wiley.

Stephen, T. (1984a). A symbolic-exchange framework for the development of intimate relationships. *Human Relations, 37,* 393-408.

Stephen, T. (1984b). Symbolic interdependence and post-break-up distress: A reformulation of the attachment construct. *Journal of Divorce, 8,* 1-16.

Stephen, T. (1986). Communication and interdependence in geographically separated relationships. *Human Communication Research, 13,* 191-210.

Stephen, T., & Markman, H. (1983). Assessing the development of relationships: A new measure. *Family Process, 22,* 15-25.

Sueda, K., & Wiseman, R. (1992). Embarrassment remediation in Japan and the United States. *International Journal of Intercultural Relations, 16,* 159-173.

Tangney, J. P. (1992). Situational determinants of shame and guilt in young adulthood. *Personality and Social Psychology Bulletin, 18,* 199-206.

Tedeschi, J. T. (1990). Self-presentation and social influence: An interactionist perspective. In M. J. Cody & M. L. McLaughlin (Eds.), *The psychol-*

ogy of tactical communication (pp. 310-323). Clevedon, England: Multilingual Matters.

Tedeschi, J., & Riess, M. (1981). Verbal strategies in impression management. In C. Antaki (Ed.), *The psychology of ordinary explanations of social behavior* (pp. 271-309). New York: Academic Press.

Ting-Toomey, S. (1988). Intercultural conflict styles: A face negotiation theory. In Y. Y. Kim & W. B. Gudykunst (Eds.), *Theories in intercultural communication* (pp. 213-238). Newbury Park, CA: Sage.

Tracy, K. (1990). The many faces of facework. In H. Giles & W. P. Robinson (Eds.), *Handbook of language and social psychology* (pp. 209-226). New York: John Wiley.

Watzlawick, P., Beavin, J., & Jackson, D. D. (1967). *Pragmatics of human communication*. New York: W. W. Norton.

Weinberg, M. S. (1968). Embarrassment: Its variable and invariable aspects. *Social Forces, 46,* 382-388.

Weiner, B., Amirkhan, J., Folkes, V. S., & Verette, J. A. (1987). An attributional analysis of excuse giving: Studies of a naive theory of emotion. *Journal of Personality and Social Psychology, 52,* 316-324.

Weiner, B., Figueroa-Muñoz, A., & Kakihara, C. (1991). The goals of excuses and communication strategies related to causal perceptions. *Personality and Social Psychology Bulletin, 17,* 4-13.

Weiner, B., & Handel, S. (1985). Anticipated emotional consequences of causal communications and reported communication strategy. *Developmental Psychology, 21,* 102-107.

Weinstein, E. A. (1969). The development of interpersonal competence. In D. A. Goslin (Ed.), *Handbook of socialization theory and research* (pp. 753-775). Chicago: Rand McNally.

Wiemann, J. M. (1977). Explication and test of a model of communicative competence. *Human Communication Research, 3,* 195-213.

Wilmot, W. W., Carbaugh, D. A., & Baxter, L. A. (1985). Communicative strategies used to terminate romantic relationships. *Western Journal of Speech Communication, 49,* 204-216.

Wood, J. T. (1982). Communication and relational culture: Bases for the study of human relationships. *Communication Quarterly, 30,* 75-83.

Yirmiya, N., & Weiner, B. (1986). Perceptions of controllability and anticipated anger. *Cognitive Development, 1,* 273-280.

Index

About the Authors

William R. Cupach received his Ph.D. in communication arts and sciences from the University of Southern California in 1981. He is currently a Professor in the Department of Communication at Illinois State University, Normal. The topic of relational competence is the central theme of his research, and currently he is exploring how individuals manage awkward, difficult, and challenging interactions in interpersonal relationships. He currently serves as Associate Editor for the communication section of the *Journal of Social and Personal Relationships*. His scholarly work has appeared in various journals, including *Human Communication Research, Journal of Social and Personal Relationships, Communication Monographs, Communication Quarterly, Journal of Language and Social Psychology, International Journal of Intercultural Relations,* and the *Western Journal of Communication*. He is coauthor, with Brian

Spitzberg, of *Interpersonal Communication Competence* (in the Sage Series on Interpersonal Communication) and the *Handbook of Interpersonal Competence Research*. Recently, he and Spitzberg completed an edited volume of essays titled *The Dark Side of Interpersonal Communication*.

Sandra Metts received her Ph.D. in communication research from the University of Iowa in 1983. She is a Professor in the Department of Communication at Illinois State University, Normal, where she teaches interpersonal communication, intercultural communication, language, and research methods. Her research interests focus on the management of problematic social and relational episodes, including embarrassment, relational disengagement, deception, relational transgressions, and sexual communication. She is coauthor, with Valerian Derlega, Sandra Petronio, and Stephen Margulis, of another book in the **Sage Series on Close Relationships**, *Self-Disclosure*. Her work has also appeared in a variety of journals, including *Communication Monographs, Human Communication Research, Journal of Social and Personal Relationships*, and *Western Journal of Communication*, as well as in many edited volumes, such as the *Handbook of Interpersonal Communication; Communication Yearbook 13; Studying Interpersonal Interaction; Theoretical Perspectives on Relationship Loss; AIDS: A Communication Perspective; The Communication of Social Support: Messages, Interactions, Relationships, and Community;* and *The Dark Side of Interpersonal Communication*.